QUALITY EDUCATION AS
A CONSTITUTIONAL RIGHT

To
Daniel Reelbock,
I hope you enjoy these
essays and find them
instructive.
Many thanks,
Bob Moses
4/7/2011

QUALITY EDUCATION AS A CONSTITUTIONAL RIGHT

Creating a Grassroots Movement
to Transform Public Schools

Edited by Theresa Perry,
Robert P. Moses, Joan T. Wynne,
Ernesto Cortés Jr., and Lisa Delpit

Beacon Press
Boston

BEACON PRESS
25 Beacon Street
Boston, Massachusetts 02108-2892
www.beacon.org

Beacon Press books
are published under the auspices of
the Unitarian Universalist Association of Congregations.

13   12   11   10   8   7   6   5   4   3   2   1

This book is printed on acid-free paper that meets the uncoated paper
ANSI/NISO specifications for permanence as revised in 1992.

Text design and composition by Wilsted & Taylor Publishing Services

Library of Congress Cataloging-in-Publication Data
Quality education as a constitutional right : creating a grassroots movement to
transform public schools / Theresa Perry [et al.]
p. cm.
Includes bibliographical references.
ISBN 978-0-8070-3282-4 (paperback : alk. paper) 1. Educational equalization—
United States. 2. Affirmative action programs—Law and legislation—United States.
3. Mainstreaming in education—United States. 4. Educational innovations—United
States. I. Perry, Theresa.
LC213.2.Q83 2010
379.2'6—dc22   2009046831

CONTENTS

The Historical and Contemporary Foundations for Robert Moses's Call to Make Quality Education a Constitutionally Guaranteed Right

Theresa Perry

It was a chilly day in March. March 11, 2005, to be exact. They came from all over the country—from the Mississippi Delta; from Los Angeles and Oakland California; New Haven and New Orleans; Denver, Colorado; Cambridge and Boston; Miami and Chicago; and the list goes on. They were established scholars and venerable civil rights icons—Charlie Cobb, Dave Dennis, Curtis Muhammad, James Comer, Jeannie Oakes, Charles Payne, Lisa Delpit, and Vincent Harding, to name a few. They came from local communities, large and small, rural and urban. They were ordinary people, individuals who had already spent a lifetime working for social justice—teachers, preachers, organizers, community leaders—whose names were known only by people whose lives they had touched, not once, but over and over again. And there were the young people, members of the hip-hop generation, some the sons and daughters of the sixties generation, others still in middle and high school. They came because, like previous generations, they had the fire for justice in their bones. They all came because of a call, a shout out, an e-mail sent by Robert P. "Bob" Moses, a hero of the civil rights movement, formerly a field secretary for the Student Nonviolent Coordinating Committee (SNCC), one of the organizers of Mississippi Freedom Summer and the Mississippi Freedom Democratic Party.

It was more than fifty years since the landmark *Brown v. Board of Education* decision, more than forty years since the passage of the Civil Rights Act of 1964, and yet equal educational opportunity for Black and Brown children had yet to be achieved. In the public, the conversation about equal educational opportunity for Black and Brown children, in newspapers, in academic journals and conferences, in public forums and community meetings, was a cacophony. Perhaps it should not even be called a conversation; at most it was a series of disconnected assertions.

"If the privileged can have choice, so should Black people; that's why I should support vouchers and charters."

"Charter schools will save public education."

"Charters are an attempt to privatize public education."

"Charter schools outperform regular public schools because they have a self-selected group of students."

"If Asian students can achieve in urban schools, then why can't Black students? It must be their culture. They don't value education."

"Money won't solve anything. Just look at how poorly Black and Brown students perform in schools that are well financed."

"Let's scrap No Child Left Behind."

"NCLB has at least forced us to see the disparities in outcomes and put some teachers and districts on notice that they are responsible for the achievement of all children."

"All we are doing in urban schools is teaching to get students to pass the test. The buildings are falling apart in urban and rural schools."

"There are few if any AP classes in math, science, or history taught in most urban schools."

"The problem is the teacher unions."

And so it goes.

They came on that chilly March day because of a call, a shout out, an e-mail, because they desperately wanted a way make sense of the cacophony, to have an organizing cry. They wanted a radical response to the undisputed reality—that schools were not working for Black, Brown, and poor children; that these children were not getting a quality education.

They came because the call offered the possibility of hope for people and organizations, the opportunity to move beyond piecemeal solutions, accusations, and small inconsequential fights, the opportunity to think about education in a bold way. They came because the call seemed to open a way for people from different positions to work together to challenge the country in the same way that the civil rights movement had challenged the county to fulfill its democratic promise.

The call they heeded was this: to build a grassroots movement to amend the Constitution to make quality education a constitutionally guaranteed right.

In calling for the formation of a movement to amend the Constitution to make quality education an enumerated right, Bob Moses was once again claiming and situating himself in the over two-hundred-year-old African American tradition of seeing education as inextricably linked to freedom and citizenship.

Because of the extraordinary work of African Americanist historians, children's literature authors, humanities and social science scholars, children and adults now have access to arresting images of what African Americans, during slavery, in the midst of the Civil War, and during Reconstruction, were willing to do get an education. We have images of African Americans attending pit schools—holes dug in the ground, covered over with branches, that served both as a way station for people trying to escape slavery and as schools for enslaved Africans learning to read. In our mind's eye, we can see the African American woman who hid the primer in her bosom, waiting for time when she could surreptitiously learn how to read from the young child in her charge, by asking what she had learned in school that day.

We are moved by images of African American soldiers during the Civil War, holding classes in their hospital beds after they had been injured, or images of them standing guard with a book in one hand and a gun in the other. We think about the young children who during slavery, one by one, with their books wrapped in paper went into the house of the teacher who was operating a secret school, in order to learn how to read. And we are often brought to tears with the story of Papa Dallas, who when he was asked what happened to his burnt-out eyes, told his granddaughter the story of how his master had thrown lye in his eyes when he was caught reading, ending his story with the exhortation to his granddaughter to tell this story to future generations so they could remember and continue to fight for an education.

We recall the description contained in the May 1953 edition of

Paul Robeson's newspaper *Freedom* in "Stories For Children: Schools Sprang Up in the South After Civil War" and in James D. Anderson's *The Education of Blacks in the South, 1860–1935* of how, in response to the generals' decision to close the school system they had established for African Americans in Louisiana during the war, African Americans developed a petition "thirty feet long . . . [with] the signatures and marks . . . of more than ten thousand Negroes.[1] The petition stated, "Tax us. We'll pay for it. If the military can't pay for it and the Freedman's Bureau can't pay for it, put a tax on us. We'll pay for it."[2]

As arresting and important as these images and narratives are, they should not obscure another equally important reality. For even as African Americans engaged in these monumental acts, they knew that these collective acts, motivated by their shared beliefs about the power of education, were not sufficient. African Americans took their intense desire for an education, their understanding of its meaning, their willingness to build schools for themselves, to tax themselves in order to provide free education to all of their children, and transformed them into an educational movement to make education an enumerated right at the state and federal levels.

According to Heather Williams,

> Alongside the traditional civil rights of suffrage and jury service, [African Americans] proposed a new right—the right to attend school. . . . [Employing] the literacy they possessed and realizing the limits of their self-taught literacy, they urged the federal government to acknowledge and protect their right to an education. Simultaneously, they appealed to state governments to provide public schooling. They shaped their own desire for schooling into a right that they believed warranted government protection.[3]

In the antebellum period, African Americans used familiar organizing strategies to develop a movement to make education a protected right. They took the issue to African American conventions, wrote articles and editorials in newspapers, held forums, created educational organizations, gave speeches, and eventually, in alliance with radical Republicans at the Southern Conventions, wrote the right to an education into state constitutions, a right that remained even as African Americans for over a century after Reconstruction would be denied an education. As Du Bois uttered decades ago, "public education at public expense in the South was essentially a Negro idea." Thus, Bob Moses's 2005 call for us to organize a movement to demand that the Constitution be amended to make quality education a constitutionally guaranteed right is but the latest iteration of African Americans' nineteenth-century struggle to make public education a right protected by the government. At the beginning of the twenty-first century, the issue is not education in general, but quality education.

As Charlie Cobb has noted, the movement to make quality education a constitutionally protected right is in its infancy. We don't have an agreement of what constitutes quality education, nor does there seem to be a clear pathway to a constitutional amendment guaranteeing quality education. Notwithstanding, since Moses's call, the notion of quality education as a civil or constitutional right has been taken up by individuals and groups all over the country, often with opposing ideological positions, from individuals who use the term to support their advocacy for vouchers, to Congressman Jesse Jackson Jr., who proposed a resolution (H.J. Resolution 29) in March of 2009 for a constitutional amendment reading

> Section 1. All persons shall enjoy the right to a public education of equal high quality.
> Section 2. The Congress shall have power to enforce and implement this article by appropriate legislation.

It is our hope that this book will be used to provoke discussion and debate in local communities and to support organizers in their efforts to find answers to these questions—what constitutes quality education, and what are the legislative routes towards getting the government to encode quality education as a protected right?

The book begins with an introductory essay by Linda Mizell. We noted that in early days after slavery, African Americans developed a movement to demand that the government protect their right to an education. Mizell provides us with an example of how this occurred in Florida in the early days of emancipation, during Reconstruction, and during the progressive era. According to Mizell, African Americans saw

> education as *not simply a civil right or even as a human right, but as a divine right.* For them, there was little distinction between political work, social uplift work, and education activism—*all* of it was God's work. . . . In a very real sense, every African American organization or institution of the period was an educational one—that is, with rare exception, no matter what the organization's primary purpose, be it social, political, civic, cultural or fraternal, education was central to its mission and its work." Mizell's essay challenges us to bring these understandings to our contemporary organizing efforts.

In developing the Algebra Project, Bob envisioned young people as math literacy workers, who, like the SNCC workers of the sixties, would be the shock troops, demanding something of themselves and of the adults working in and making policy for schools and school systems. Charles Payne's interview of the Baltimore Algebra Project students stands in stark contrast to the popular narrative about young Black youth as a group who don't value education. The young people talk about their activism, give us details about their campaign for quality education, their sit-ins, mock trial of the state superintendent, and their systematic work with middle school students taking algebra. This was and is Bob Moses's vision for the Algebra Project, the essence of what he learned from Ella Baker. It would be the youth who would lead the way.

The essays in part II by Jeannie Oakes, Bob Moses, Ernesto Cortés, and Imani Perry are designed to help us grapple with the following questions: Can the Constitution guarantee quality education? What are the routes that can lead us in that direction? What is the role of organizers in a legal fight? What coalitions are necessary? How can the fight for quality education be waged at the state, city, and federal levels? What new understanding of the law can be employed that will be likely to succeed at this time, when we have the first African American president in the White House and a Democratic Congress? How might the thirteenth amendment be used to support congressional legislation to encode into law and guarantee quality education?

Part III of this book begins with essays by two exemplary educators, Alicia Carroll, a kindergarten teacher, and Kimberly N. Parker, a high school teacher. These essays, along with essays by Joan T. Wynne and Janice Giles on Bob Moses's summer math program for high school students, and Lisa Delpit on culturally responsive teaching, should prompt rich conversations and debates about what constitutes quality education. Can we codify a definition of quality? All of the essays in this section are meant to suggest that as we organize to make quality education a constitutionally guaranteed right, we have to be about the business of instantiating excellence in the meantime. The essays provide a starting point for local communities to begin conversations, grounded in practice, about what constitutes quality education. Over the two decades of the school reform movement, foundation money has supported school systems and school reform and policy organizations to discuss, propose, and enact visions of education for Black and Brown communities. It is time for our communities to begin to have these conversations. Tentative and ever-evolving answers to these questions will inform organizing efforts to make quality education a constitutionally guaranteed right.

For those of us committed to transforming sharecropper education to quality education, this is both a complicated and hopeful time. It is complicated because school reform has become a top-down phenomenon. We have seen the increasing disenfranchisement of local communities in decisions about schools and in discussion about the contents of public education. And as the public sphere has become demonized, so have public schools. Bob Moses has opined that we seem content to move students around and create ways for a few kids to get a better education, rather than trying to transform the system as a whole.

It is a hopeful time because there are stirrings of a renewed sense that government must play a role in addressing historic inequities. Youth are organizing, and disenfranchised communities are demanding quality education. While there are over forty state lawsuits related to the equalization of education, we have a better understanding of what has to happen, even if the plaintiffs are victorious, for equity to be actualized in schools.

President Obama's victory on a campaign of hope opens imaginative possibilities. Imagine if President Obama talked straight to the nation, and specifically to the children and families in urban and rural communities, telling them, "I know I am asking you to pursue excellence in a context of inequities." What if he said, "I know that in some of your schools you don't have libraries, auditoriums, gyms, computers. But you still have to work hard and study hard. And I promise you, I will try and make it so that by the end of my second term all children have what they need to achieve in their schools"? What if he said that he was ushering in the next stage of the struggle for quality education? Imagine President Obama convening a working group of educators, youth and adult organizers, legal and educational scholars, charging them with developing an understanding of the resource requirements for an education in the twenty-first century and exploring how to encode these requirements in federal legislation that would make it a right for every child to have access to these resources in his or her school. Or to state it differently, what if he spearheaded the development of legislation that required states to deliver on these requirements with an accompanying authorization for federal funding to assist local and state governmental units meet their legislative responsibilities? When we heard that the money for school construction was being taken out of the stimulus package, many of us were disappointed. However, the real issue is that there is no federal requirement that the state or localities provide a floor of resources for our schools, urban or rural.

We all know that President Obama is the product of a White American mother and a Kenyan father, and that he lived and attended private schools in Indonesia and Hawaii. However, as a young adult, in his search for identity, he chose to identify as African American. He moved to Chicago, where Black means African American, organized on the south side of Chicago in the African American community, married an African American woman, and attended an Afrocentric African American church for close to twenty years. In these environments, he learned and gained facility in the use of Black language and in Black cultural practices, formal and informal, which have been on full display in his speeches and interactions during the campaign and since his election as president. We remember the fist bump that he and his wife, Michelle, shared on stage and his response to the cashier at the restaurant in Washington, D.C, when, after he was asked if he needed change, he said, "We straight." We recall how in a campaign speech to a largely Black audience, he effectively used words that Spike Lee had attributed to Malcolm in the movie *Malcom X*. He said, "They're trying to bamboozle you. It's the same old okey-doke. Y'all know about okey-doke, right?" In speaking about the extravagant lifestyles of bank executives, he excoriated them for living "high on the hog." In his speeches, he used Black rhetorical style—repetition, rhythm, and actual phrases that are reminiscent of the words of Dr. Martin Luther King Jr.—and the preaching style of Black ministers generally: "They said this day would never come. They said our sights were set too high. They said this country was too divided." Having located himself inside this tradition, he spoke in a way that had resonance for Black Americans particularly and at the same time spoke to all Americans.

Having chosen an African American identity, President Obama will, we hope, also claim his place in the African American tradition of seeing education as a path to freedom and will use the office of president to support these strivings.

Now is the time for ordinary people to be heard, to demand that the government at all levels (federal, state, and local) guarantee quality education, and for ordinary people to offer robust descriptions of quality education, ones that can be encoded in law and monitored by appropriate governmental agencies as well as an organized and vigilant public.

NOTES

1. Paul Robeson, "Stories for Children: Schools Sprang Up in South after Civil War," *Freedom* (May 1953).

2. James D. Anderson, *The Education of Blacks in the South, 1860–1935* (Chapel Hill: University of North Carolina Press, 1988), 9–10.

3. Heather Andrea Williams, *Self-taught: African American Education in Slavery and Freedom* (Chapel Hill: University of North Carolina Press, 2007), 68–69.

4. For other books that discuss African Americans' struggle for literacy and an education during enslavement, the Civil War, and Reconstruction, see Janet Cornelius, *When I Can Read My Title Clear: Literacy, Slavery, and Religion in the Antebellum South* (Columbia: University of South Carolina Press, 1991), and Christopher M. Spann, *From Cotton Field to Schoolhouse: African American Education in Mississippi, 1862–1875* (Chapel Hill: University of North Carolina Press, 2009).

"The Holy Cause of Education"

Lessons from the History of
a Freedom-Loving People

Linda Mizell

Oh, we have paid for our children's place in the world again,
and again.

—*Sherley Ann Williams,* Dessa Rose

Despite centuries of evidence to the contrary, the belief that African Americans don't value education has become so pervasive that it shapes policy and practice in all areas of school reform. Underlying these perceptions of both the past and the present is the basic assumption of White largesse and Black neediness—that African Americans come to the enterprise of education as beggars, bringing nothing to the table—no resources, no expertise, no capacity, no ambition. Yet the work of historians and other scholars of African American education such as James D. Anderson, Michelle Foster, Vanessa Siddle Walker, Valinda Littlefield, Curtis and Vivian Morris Gunn, and numerous others tells a very different story.

It is a story, in fact countless stories, of African American communities building educational institutions—what James Weldon Johnson called "main centers of pride and affection"—and providing these institutions with every means of support that the communities' resources would allow, far above and beyond tax dollars, while challenging White supremacy and the state-imposed inequalities of separate schools.

Let me note here that I quite consciously use the term educational institutions, rather than schools. Historical research on African American education has focused primarily and appropriately on the development of public schools, and for well over a century, schooling has been an ideological battleground in our struggles to gain access to the rights of equal citizenship under the law; however, the historical struggle for equal access to educational opportunity was not limited to schools, but rather was waged in every sphere in which African Americans recognized the possibilities for expanding their knowledge of the world. Emerging scholarship has begun to shift our attention to the complex relationships between schools (both public and private) and institutions such as libraries, orphanages, reformatories, and quasi-public institutions such as YMCAs in early-twentieth-century African American communities.

This body of work does a number of things, but there are two in particular that I'd like to emphasize. First, it challenges, in unequivocal terms, the assumption about African Americans not caring about education, and in fact makes the case that no people cared more, literally risking life and limb in order to attain it. Historian David Tyack argues that "during the nineteenth century no group in the United States had a greater faith in the equalizing power of schooling or a clearer understanding of the democratic promise of public education than did black Americans." In the groundbreaking work *Remembering Slavery*, Tonea Stewart tells the moving story of Papa Dallas, who was beaten and blinded by an overseer for trying to learn to read; rather than lamenting his fate, Papa Dallas used the story to encourage his descendents "to go all the way through school, as far as you can" and to "tell all the children my story."

Second, this scholarship challenges the perception of education in general and schooling in particular as something that was given to African Americans. To the contrary, in one way or another, most White students quite literally owe their own educational attainment to the struggles of previous generations of African Americans. Anderson argues that in the nineteenth century, African Americans "were the first among native southerners to wage a campaign for universal public education." And in the twentieth century, such initiatives as the federal student loan program grew out of the Southern-based, Black-led freedom movement, otherwise known as the civil rights movement, which paved the way for President Lyndon Johnson's War on Poverty.

These findings resonate in my own research on the development of Black education in late-nineteenth-century and early-twentieth-century Florida, when African Americans took up what they called "the holy cause of education."

In 1868, Florida became one of only a handful of states that encoded education into its constitution as a civil right, notably "without distinction or preference" on the basis of race. While the new constitution did not explicitly prohibit segregation, it is significant that it did not require it, either, due largely to the efforts of the leadership of the African Methodist Episcopal (and, to a lesser extent, Baptist) churches who formed a powerful legislative bloc. Ministers exhorted their congregations to register to vote and to run for office, in service of this "holy cause of education." Of the eighteen African Americans elected to the state constitutional convention, six were laymen and four were ministers in the AME Church.

In 1869, under pressure exerted by this same bloc, the legislature voted to create the first operative statewide system of free common schools (earlier attempts had been funded, quite literally, on the backs of enslaved African Americans—in 1850, the state assembly mandated that slaves seized by the court were to be sold and proceeds of the sale given to the newly established common school fund). Through gubernatorial appointment, supervision of schools in three of Florida's largest (and Blackest) counties was vested in AME ministers; in addition, Jonathan Gibbs, an African American Dartmouth-educated Presbyterian minister who served as both secretary of state and as supervisor of public instruction, was the first (and for many decades *only*) Florida superintendent of any race to address the National Education Association. In his 1874 report, Gibbs declared, "God is on the side of the schoolhouse!" These men (and the visionary women whose names tend to go unrecorded) saw education as *not simply a civil right or even as a human right, but as a divine right.* For them, there was little distinction between political work, social uplift work, and education activism—*all* of it was God's work.

In 1885, with a Democrat in the governor's office and a White Democratic majority in place, Florida's Reconstruction-era constitution was replaced by a new document that successfully undermined, if not dismantled, the progressive legislation of the previous generation; through such measures as the enactment of a poll tax as a requirement for voting, the legislature sought to disenfranchise the last remnants of Black political activism within the state government by incorporating White supremacy into statute and law.

W. N. Sheats, who in another decade would begin his rise to national prominence as "Florida's little giant of education," drafted the language of Section 12, which declared that "White and colored children shall not be taught in the same school, but impartial provision shall be made for both," though it would soon be clear that the allocation of resources would be far from impartial. In addition, it mandated that the state superintendent of education be an elected office; since the majority of African Americans were effectively barred from voting, a similar mandate for the county superintendent posts virtually guaranteed that none would hold such offices. While the legislature made most offices elective, the governor's authority to appoint county commissioners was continued, thus assuring White control of the Black belt counties.

Thus, at the dawn of the Progressive era, the most pressing challenge to Black education activists was to hold the state accountable to its promise of "impartial provision," despite the purging of African Americans from political office and the consequent diminution in political agency. Even as the social and political status of African Americans continued to deteriorate throughout the South, Florida's Black leaders continued to agitate "for justice and equality in civil, political and business relations in life." In a move that shook White Republicans, Black leaders called a "state conference of colored men" in Gainesville in February 1884, at which they debated the establishment of a racially integrated independent party. Topping the list of six recommendations was a reaffirmation of the primacy of education in the Black political agenda: "We want increased facilities of common school education and the higher branches so as to be able to reduce the high rate of illiteracy which the last census shows to exist among our people in this state." In the debate leading up to formulation of these recommendations, speakers made the case for slavery reparations as sound public policy, arguing that tax-supported Black schools were "a quid pro quo" for uncompensated Black labor.

What was true for these earlier generations was true for succeeding ones—consistently, throughout each stage of struggle, African Americans made few distinctions between social, political, and educational activism. In a very real sense, every African American organization or institution of the period was an educational one—that is, with rare exception, no matter what the organization's primary purpose, be it social, political, civic, cultural, or fraternal, education was central to its mission and its work. The Friendship Garden Club, a Black women's civic organization, planted flowers on the grounds of local schools and opened Miami's first Black library in a storefront owned by one of its members. In Fort Lauderdale, Reverend Ivory Mizell began a library in the office of the Dixie Court Housing Project so that Black children would have access to books.

One of the goals of Jacksonville's League for Democracy, organized after World War I by Black veterans, was to secure "a just, fair and unprejudiced record of the achievements of the colored military in the histories used in the public schools." They expected that this counternarrative would help further the struggle "against the arch enemies of the race—lynching, jim-crowing, disenfranchisement, discrimination, inequality in educational advantages as well as justice in the courts and economic and industrial freedom." As Joyce A. Hanson notes in her biography of Florida educator, activist, and clubwoman Mary McLeod Bethune, "Educating children *was* the essence of race work."

Activists consistently connected the rights of citizenship to support for education. In a 1919 editorial, the Pensacola *Colored Citizen* opined: "In the matter of schools, there should be a large registration in order that [Black voters] might vote to carry the bond issue, so that the schools of the city can be put on a first class basis." In that same year, the Civic League for Colored People of St. Petersburg pooled its resources to help nearly four hundred African Americans pay their poll taxes, in order to "make efforts for a longer school term by every man paying his poll tax, that our strength may be considered by the school board when lining up for the next term of school."

In April 1919, civil rights activists assembled in Ocala, in numbers that were surprising even to attendees, to form a statewide Negro Uplift Association (NUA). Delegates to the conference represented chapter and affiliated organizations from all over the state, counting ministers, lodge officials, former city council members, teachers, and businessmen among their number. The conference identified "adequate provisions for education and better protection and care for delinquent children" as central to its platform. N. B. Young, the embattled president of Florida Agricultural and Mechanical College for Negroes, was a keynote speaker, and Ortiz writes that his "militant address" on the failure of the South's segregated school system "set the note for the conference."

While the anti-lynching struggle was arguably the single most urgent issue among African Americans—between 1900 and 1930,

Florida had the highest per capita rate of lynching in the South—the conference's anti–Jim Crow resolution also included pleas for "a longer school term, and a colored superintendent for the State Industrial School," the tax-supported facility where African American boys made up the majority of inmates.

At the same time that Florida's African American male leaders were pursuing a political intervention into the plight of incarcerated boys, the State Federation of Colored Women's Clubs was engaged in building, staffing, and funding a facility for delinquent girls, one of several around the country established by African American clubwomen in the early twentieth century.

Under the leadership of such women as Bethune and through the efforts of ordinary men and women who raised money, registered voters, planted gardens, and did whatever was necessary to create systems of support for Florida's Black children and the communities that sustained them: in all these ways, and more, African Americans demonstrated what Stephanie Shaw has described as a collective "consciousness of kind," one which engaged women, men, and children in "thoughtful, deliberate processes of community building that combined the construction of schools, libraries, orphanages, churches and other institutions with efforts to develop human consciousness" —and in the process produced "women and men who could symbolize the power and potential of the group."

Certainly, the various campaigns and initiatives launched by Florida's African American men and women to address the social and educational needs of Black children support this assertion; the treatment of delinquent Black children, for example, was as much a political issue as it was a social service issue, one that could not be adequately addressed without a well-organized campaign that focused on legislative action *and* on the creation of institutions—both in terms of brick-and-mortar facilities and in the sociological sense of establishing a structured pattern of relationships that would be accepted as a fundamental part of Florida's culture. The efforts by such individuals and organizations certainly speaks to the regard in which Black Floridians held every aspect of educational opportunity and to their enduring faith in their own capacity to create avenues of access.

In *Dessa Rose,* Sherley Ann Williams's 1986 novel set in the antebellum South, the title character muses on the challenges of slavery and of freedom and on the power of the written word in determining her fate. Like Papa Dallas exacting a promise from his granddaughter to tell his story, Dessa repeats her harrowing story to her grandchildren and the other children of their settlement: "This why I have it wrote down," she says, "why I has the child say it back. . . . *this* the childrens have heard from our own lips." The novel (and its recent stage adaptation) offers a profound reflection on the perception among freedmen and freedwomen, as characterized by Anderson, of literacy as "a contradiction of oppression." Equally important, it is an affirmation of the necessity, as our wise elder brother Vincent Harding frequently reminds us, of claiming, reclaiming, owning, sharing, *and learning from* our historical memory of African Americans' centuries-long struggle for education and literacy.

Forty acres and a mule have come to symbolize the hopes, aspirations and unfulfilled promise of American freedom; I'm convinced, however, that an equally powerful and appropriate symbol is the schoolhouse. The Quality Education as a Civil Right campaign calls us to join, in Brother Vincent's words, "a movement older and deeper than any one life, any one generation," that has always had literacy for freedom at its core. It is a movement with an inclusive vision, one that calls for people from poor communities, immigrant communities, and communities of color—those who have been most excluded from access to this most fundamental of civil and human rights—to be at its forefront. It is a movement that calls for us to build and sustain alliances that erase boundaries, real or imagined, to collectively engaging in the practice of freedom.

Our history offers us lessons in how such movements have been envisioned, formulated, and actualized. It also offers us a sacred legacy of hope and possibility.

And we are claiming it.

PART I

Organizing

The Youth Shall Lead the Way

Miss Baker's Grandchildren

An Interview with the Baltimore Algebra Project

Charles M. Payne

It took about 25 minutes to get the first Baltimore City School Board meeting of the year . . . started but it took only two minutes to push the meeting to the brink of complete chaos.

—Baltimore City Paper, *January 17, 2007*

I remember when I wouldn't even participate in class. Now they have me on radio shows and all that. Yeah, it's just really, really fun, yeah.

—*Chris Goodman, Baltimore Algebra Project*

For Bob Moses, one of the turning points of the struggle in Mississippi was the moment when the demand for the right to vote came from the disenfranchised themselves. From that viewpoint, it is important that the demand to treat quality education as a right of citizenship come from students and parents. Perhaps the clearest illustration of that is the history of the Baltimore Algebra Project (BAP), another iteration in the long tradition of hell-raising young Black people. If it were the 1930s, they would have been part the Young Negroes' Cooperative League, forbidding membership to anyone over the age of thirty because people of such advanced age were presumed to be out of touch politically. In the 1940s, they would have been the Southern Negro Youth Congress, about as far to the left as an organization could be in the South of that time, advocating that Black youth stop leaving the South and do whatever was needed to transform it. In the 1980s, they would have been the Black Student Leadership Network, an alliance of several activist initiatives that laid the foundation of the network of freedom schools the Children's Defense Fund now operates. The most direct linkage, of course, is to the Student Nonviolent Coordinating

Committee (SNCC). There is one problem the Baltimore Algebra Project shares with all of its predecessors. It is easy to be misled when looking at them—to see the hell-raising and thinks that's all that's there. Nothing could be further from the truth. They are a part of one of the most thoughtful, self-aware and other-aware traditions of American activism—they are "organizing in the spirit of Ella," to borrow a phrase from Bob Moses.

An icon in some activist circles, Ella Baker is still not well known to broader publics. Suffice it to say that she had an enormous impact on the civil rights movement and on American activism more broadly. For over forty years, starting in the late 1920s, she was on the cutting edge of Black activism, which meant socialist organizations and economic cooperatives during the Depression, the NAACP in the forties, and the Southern Christian Leadership Conference in the fifties. Perhaps her crowning achievement was the role she played in the creation of SNCC, which in turn transformed American activism. It took the movement into the rural South; it pushed older civil rights organizations into more direct action; it was a major influence on Students for Democratic Society, as well as the Black Panther Party and the Black studies movement. Perhaps no other organization did as much to define the direct action, confrontational politics that came to define the sixties as did the Student Nonviolent Coordinating Committee. Its political style reflected the lessons Miss Baker had learned from a lifetime of activism: work for the long haul; don't put too much stock in leaders or their charisma; build group-centered leadership, not leader-centered groups; develop leadership among the uncredentialed, including poor people, women, and youth. "The salvation of the world is in its youth," she said, ". . . hence it is of paramount importance that the trend of youth's thoughts be guided."[1] Miss Baker mentored a long list of important activists, Bob Moses among them.

Moses is one direct link between BAP and SNCC. Betty Garman Robinson, one of BAP's adult allies, also worked for SNCC in Mississippi, and she helped pull BAP together in the early 1990s. Initially, BAP trained teachers to use Algebra Project pedagogy. By 2000, enough middle school students had learned math in the Algebra Project and graduated to high school that they could start to share what they knew by tutoring other students. Tutors were paid ten dollars an hour for their work. Jay Gillen, another of their adult allies, saw this as a way of getting youngsters immediately involved in the information economy, a way to make the point early on that rewards flow to those who know more.

In the 2002 school year, the Baltimore City school system, pleased with the work the tutors were doing, wrote the project into its budget. It was written into the budget again for 2003, but when the time came, the system didn't actually have the money. Looking back, one suspects that had city and state officials understood how much trouble that one little decision was going to bring their way, they would have raised that money even if it had meant having a bake sale.

These were not simply young people running a tutoring program; these were young people with a sense of history running a tutoring program—which, as they say, is the difference between lightning and the lightning bug. When something goes awry, they have models for interpreting it, which others would not have; they have models for reacting, which others would not have. Trying to find out what had happened to the money, they started studying the city school budget and learned that Baltimore City schools were in deficit to the tune of $58 million. They also learned that the state was culpable to a significant degree. In 2000, a circuit court ruling had ordered the state of Maryland to live up to its constitutional mandate to provide adequate funding and ordered it to pay an additional $200 million to $265 million to Baltimore City schools annually. The state has responded slowly, claiming that it doesn't have the money and that Baltimore City would mismanage the funds if it had them. By BAP's calculations, the amount owed under the ruling has since grown to $1.05 billion.

Once the young people learned about underfunding, it ignited a war of words between them and city and state officials. Funding became the chief focus of BAP's advocacy committee; they held rallies, protests, teach-ins, and strikes. "No Education, No Life!" became their rallying cry. To dramatize it, at one of their rallies protesting school closings, over one hundred students—one account says four hundred—lay down in the street as if dead. In October 2004, they showed up at a state Board of Education meeting with plans to arrest the state secretary of education. "Today, Nancy Grasmick," called out Lorne Francis, then a seventeen-year-old BAP spokesperson, "I place you under citizen's arrest. You are charged with two counts of failure to obey a court order and 85,000 counts of reckless endangerment," referring to the 85,000 students in the city's schools. The youth pretty much took over the meeting, to the point where the state board members walked out of their own meeting.

Student walkouts and strikes began in the winter and early spring of 2004. Teachers were being laid off. There was talk that the school system might shut down completely because of cash-flow problems. Some schools locked fire exits and used pepper spray to try to prevent students from attending rallies. The largest strike rally that year involved eight hundred students gathering at City Hall and marching to the state board of education. Not coincidentally, the mayor announced the same day that since the state refused to help the city school system with its cash flow, he would offer a loan of city funds to the schools, and so the 2004 strikes were defused.

The fall of 2006 was designated as Freedom Fall, hearkening back to Freedom Summer, the summer of '64, when the Student Nonviolent Coordinating Committee invited hundreds of college students to Mississippi to help expose the racism of that state. Freedom Fall was intended "to expose Maryland's blatant racial oppression through a lack of quality education, and the unconstitutional way in which Baltimore City schools are persistently underfunded." Freedom schools, which SNCC had originated that summer, were held across the city. Students were informed about underfunding and its consequences, invited to discuss the quality of the education they were receiving, and encouraged to go back to their schools and ask teachers for class time to talk about the same issues.

Students at the Baltimore Freedom Academy were inspired to take action by BAP's militancy and by their own studies of the civil rights movement. Fifty of them occupied a stairwell in the school building on October 13, 2006, as they demanded calculators for their math classes and more textbooks. They were all suspended; some were reportedly forced to transfer to other schools. BAP representatives were banned from the building.

In 1964, Freedom Summer involved the creation of new institutions, responsive to the people, parallel to the institutions that oppressed or ignored them. The Mississippi Freedom Democratic Party was one such institution. In that spirit, the Algebra Project created the Maryland Freedom Board of Education, for which they found ample justification in Article 6 of the Maryland Constitution:

All persons invested with the Legislative or Executive pow-
ers are the Trustees of the Public, and, as such, accountable
for their conduct. Wherefore, whenever the ends of government are perverted . . . the People may, and of right, ought to
reform the old, or establish a new Government, the doctrine
of non-resistance against arbitrary power and oppression is
absurd, slavish and destructive of the good and happiness of
mankind.

At its first meeting, the board unveiled a new spending plan for
Baltimore City schools. Subsequently, with a gubernatorial election
looming, it contacted all candidates and tried to get them to take a
position on their issues. By the end of the fall, Judge Joseph Kaplan of
the circuit court ordered the city and state to work with the Algebra
Project students in developing a funding plan for the next year. Ultimately, the goal of the body is "to become the Board of Education for
the people," says its chair, Chris Goodman. According to organizer
Fernandes Harlee, "If the system doesn't work for us, we need to make
our own. We can't wait anymore."

If the young people are very conscious of themselves as historical actors, many of the officials with whom they are butting heads
seem oblivious to how much they look and sound like the power brokers of the past (and some of today's gatekeepers are Black). At one
point, a group of BAP members trying to speak to the superintendent were handcuffed by her security people. At a demonstration in
January 2005, Jay Gillen, the adult ally, was arrested as the students
were protesting at a state Board of Education meeting. Procedures
at public meetings have been changed so that it is more difficult for
BAP members to get into meetings or to say anything when they get
there. In January 2007, for example, police assaulted one student, organizer Harlee, who was waiting for a board meeting to begin. They
claimed the room was too crowded and that Fernandes had disobeyed
a police order to clear an aisle. Despite weeks of student pressure and
eyewitness accounts from teachers and students, the board refused to
condemn the brutality. Like generations of activists before them, BAP
members are learning how undemocratic and unresponsive public
institutions become when someone insists the needs of poor people
be attended to.

It goes without saying that militant youth organizations make the elders nervous. Civic leaders in Baltimore have accused BAP of engaging in activism for activism's sake; they see them as children who don't understand how complicated the world is, who want everything done overnight. Nevertheless, BAP has pushed older organizations to a more aggressive posture. Black civic groups are noticeably more outspoken about school funding issues in Baltimore than are their counterparts in other cities. As Charles Cobb observed in Mississippi during the '60s,

> Repression is the law; oppression a way of life.... Here, an idea of your own is a subversion that must be squelched; for each bit of intellectual initiative represents the threat of a probe into the why of denial. Learning here means only learning to stay in your place.... There is hope and there is dissatisfaction.... This is the generation that has silently made the vow of no more raped mothers, no more castrated fathers; that looks for an alternative to a lifetime of bent, burnt, and broken backs, minds and souls. Their creativity must be molded from the rhythm of a muttered "white son-of-a-bitch," from the roar of a hunger-bloated belly and from the stench of rain and mudwashed shacks.... What they must see is the link between a rotting shack and a rotting America.[2]

In today's Baltimore, one could rewrite that in terms of opportunities to learn being restricted by the lack of resources, by pervasive low expectations and low standards.

Obviously, Cobb was thinking in structural terms; the problems in Mississippi couldn't be reduced to prejudice and individual malice. Something much more systematic was in play. Similarly, the students in the Baltimore Algebra Project understand the starvation of the school system as just one part of larger patterns of marginalization of their communities, of larger issues about how privilege is distributed. At the same time, SNCC was very much aware that we can internalize the structures of oppression. "Every step in the fight against racism and discrimination," Cobb wrote, "was preceded by a deeper and more profound struggle that involved confronting oneself,"[3] which could mean confronting one's own fear, one's own apathy, one's own egotism. Students in BAP talk about their struggles with the need to accept criticisms, with some of their own attitudes about learning, with the struggle to develop the confidence to stand up against people who are older and more experienced than they.

For many in SNCC, parallel to the fight against negative tendencies within oneself was the fight to create and sustain community within the movement. Many of its members give some credit for its internal community to Ella Baker. "The SNCC of which I was a part," says Casey Hayden, "was nurturing, warm, familial, supportive, honest and penetrating, radical and pragmatic. I think of it as womanist. I see Ella in all of that."[4] Listening to BAP students talk about what keeps them in the group, what keeps them coming back even after high school, it is clear that they have created a very powerful community among themselves, a place where they feel accepted for who they are, a place where they can drop their normal fronts. BAP seems to attract both some of the strong students, already headed for college, and some students who have been in all kinds of trouble and seemed headed for more. They seem to have such a strong sense of community among themselves that what they did before the Algebra Project has little to do with how they interact among themselves. They are very aware of how the culture they've created among themselves differs from the more competitive, put-down culture that often exists among their peers.

The students of the Baltimore Algebra Project, then, see themselves as engaged in a struggle against a system that unfairly distributes opportunity, but they also see themselves as engaged in a struggle against backwards traits within themselves—what old people used to call hold-backs—and in a struggle to maintain supportive community among themselves. It is about as far as one can get from the mindless activism of which they have been accused.

Susan Wilcox, one of the directors of Brotherhood/Sister Sol, a New York youth agency, says the point of that organization's work is to shape a generation of youth who think, feel, dream, and act out of their own self- and world-awareness. BAP is an example of what such a generation would look like. Many people in SNCC thought of themselves as the children of Ella Baker; if so, the young people of the Baltimore Algebra Project are her grandchildren.

What follows are excerpts from an interview with several members of BAP during the summer of 2006.

INTERVIEW WITH THE
BALTIMORE ALGEBRA PROJECT

Moderator
Charles Payne

Participants

Mahogany Bosworth, Baltimore Polytechnic Institute
Chelsea Carson, Heritage High School '06, Bowie State University
Xzavier Cheatom, Heritage High School
Charnell Covert, Baltimore City College High School '05, Eugene
   Lang College
Michael Fogarty, Doris M. Johnson High School
Christopher Goodman, City College High School '06, University
   of Maryland, College Park
Fernandes Harlee, New Era Academy
Ryan Mason, MerVo (Mergenthaler Vocational High School)
Channell Parker, Baltimore Polytechnic Institute
Michele Shropshire (now Parker), Baltimore Polytechnic
   Institute '04, College of Notre Dame
Wayne Washington, Lake Clifton 425 (now Heritage High School)

MODERATOR: I want some of you to talk about impacts, the experience of being an advocate, the experience of organizing demonstrations, the experience of dealing with all the publicity. How did you get into this?

RYAN: I've been in the Algebra Project with the advocacy committee for about eight months now. Charnell did tell me about the Algebra Project because we are both members of an organization called Solvivaz Nation. I did security for one of the events and then about two months later, I came to an advocacy meeting and I just kept coming ever since.

MODERATOR: You came to an advocacy meeting. What struck you?

RYAN: I'm in a lot of different youth organizations around the city. I like to think that the advocacy committee with the Algebra Project was very proactive. I know a lot of organizations are very stagnant. They do a lot of meeting about meetings. To see around the city, my peers who are actually involved and actually doing something and actually calling people out on what they're not doing—it's hard to find that, and that's something that I found with the Algebra Project.

MODERATOR: So you found something you've been looking for. Has it had an impact on you? Do you see yourself as having been changed by it?

RYAN: Yeah. People in school called me "little Malcolm X" because I'm always talking about civil rights and Black power this, and we've got to do this and things like that and always being proactive. But being in with the Algebra Project has helped me see that there are students that are my age, who actually are interested in doing these things. You know, I'm usually seeing adults who are going after these different things. Or young adults, you know, twenty-one and over. But when you see people who are from freshmen in high school to sophomores in college, you know, it's uplifting to see that, "Okay, I'm not the only one in this." So it's actually really raised my expectations of my peers as well as myself.

XZAVIER: Yeah, I got into the Algebra Project [and] it all started with me going to Mergenthaler High School [MerVo]. Life was just very difficult at the time and it interfered with my academics and I got put out of MerVo my ninth-grade year. So they sent me to this other school and it was like going from a mansion to a cardboard box, where it's practically just nothing but you know, walls and the floor.

So I'm in there, and I'm just working hard to get out this school that's just so horrible. And somebody told me about the Algebra Project. I had scored ninety-eights on my report cards and final exams and mid-terms and stuff like that. And I was hearing about the issues with the underfunding with the schools and stuff like that. And I've seen it firsthand. So I thought, you know, I should be more active and just participate in this. Me being a hard worker, I had hopped into it. They allowed me to take that leadership position so fast, and they trusted me with it. So I'm pretty much stuck here until they have no more assignments.

CHELSEA: I was a client before I got involved with the Algebra Project. Mr. Jay Gillen was my math teacher in middle school. Sometimes I feel like he grew me into the Algebra Project, because he was just very enthusiastic about getting me involved. "Well, fill out the application and come to the training and this, this, and this." And then ever since then, I've just been actively involved in the Algebra Project.

CHRIS: I joined the Algebra Project same time Chelsea did. I was a client in the eighth grade. I really liked the experience you know, getting tutored by people who graduated from the same middle school. It was fun. So [I] worked on the bridge committee that summer and became a tutor, because if I wasn't in the Algebra Project, I would probably just play basketball all day or something like that.

WAYNE: Okay. Before I was in the project, I used to be that boy that was what they call a "blot," someone being kicked out of the house almost every three weeks and living here and living there. And had to go through problems inside the house and was in beef. Matter of fact, before I went to Lake Clifton, I was at Southwestern and a couple other schools. And I've been kicked out because of the beef that had been traveling from school to school.

So I went to Lake Clifton and I joined the Algebra Project. And the main reason why I joined it so I could be in something that let's say would keep me out of the streets for a little bit.

MODERATOR: Did you go in as a client, as a tutor?

WAYNE: Well, you start off as a client. But my main objective was to be a tutor. I didn't know about the Algebra Project until a math teacher, Miss Brown, told me that I know the math and I should just join the Algebra Project. So I went. At first it was just to get the money and to stay out of the streets. But then after a while I actually got into it. Like this is my family. It changed [me]. Like, I'm not on the street. I'm not in a whole bunch of beef now. Not just that, it made me realize what I can do inside of school and how I can help other people. And just maybe I became a leader because of the Algebra Project.

And it just helped me in so many different ways. It made me realize what I've got outside also of the Algebra Project. Like, I got closer with my family, my household family. The Algebra Project doesn't just help you as in your grades and realizing that you're good in academics and stuff like that. It also helps you as being a better person.

Like my self-esteem was way down there and came up just by being in here. Just by knowing that I can come in here and put my hand up and everybody else saying "Hi," to me, it helped a lot.

MODERATOR: Anyone else on how you got in? How and why you got in?

CHARNELL: I got in because one of my best friends recommended me. I really admire him because I thought he was really good at math. And he was actually helping me with math. And he was like, "Oh, you know that you really ought to stay in this." And I was talking to Mr. Nik [Thomas Nikundiwe] because he's one of my teachers, and I was just like, "Um, this is so amazing to me because I know you remember how bad I was when I was in class." And he was just like, "I actually don't remember you being that bad, Charnell. I remember you working really hard." I was like, "Oh. That's interesting, because my perception of my abilities were that they were inadequate." And immediately I was drawn in because it was student run. The president was a student. The vice, everything was student-run. It just amazed me, the funds and everything. I was looking at these people like "Wow, there's nothing really different from them and me. Like they're in high school, they go to Harbor, they go to City," or wherever they went. And it really enthralled me I guess.

And then shortly after I became secretary. I always thought I would never do secretarial work, but it was a whole different type of secretary. It was like, "secretary of SNCC" type of thing. And I was very mindful again, of Africans and African American history. So I always had this feeling that we were history at the Algebra Project. And I just felt really good being a part of that. And then it just kept going from there. And my math skills obviously have improved quite a bit.

But it started by somebody just seeing that I actually wasn't as bad as I thought I was at the particular time. And I'm glad that someone supported me and acknowledged that. My parents definitely did too, but I'm glad that I had someone in the project that pulled me in.

MODERATOR: Do you want to say something about how and why you got in and why did you stay in the Algebra Project?

MAHOGANY: How? Well, my first year, my algebra one teacher recommended me to be a tutor for the Algebra Project [at] Baltimore Polytechnic. And why did I stay in? More or less, I just liked tutoring. It was fun. Nice knowing that I was helping somebody and improving them, even if it was just like one or two kids. I got to tutor them, help them with their math. And I had fifth graders. They liked learning. I guess they were interested in what I was saying. Like, they actually came every Tuesday and Thursday. And they were there the whole tutoring time, waiting for their snacks and all that. And at the other site at Lemmel, I had eighth graders. At Lemmel, they came when they wanted to. Teachers made them come. I had students that they really didn't want to be there. I mean they learned. They sat there and listened but they really didn't want to be there.

CHANNELL: I worked at the Stadium School. I worked with these three boys and they were in fifth or sixth grade. And I wouldn't call them bad, but they were really difficult. They worked with another guy who didn't really challenge them. When I came . . . they knew that they were about to have a drill, a test, or a quiz. And they knew they were about to work and they would come. After a while it was to the point where, "I want to work with Channell. I want to work with Channell." And everyone would look at them as the bad boys. And that made them want to come to work even more.

These are Black Baltimore City kids [that] nobody believes in. And they're all going to get in trouble every single day. I used to have to wait like ten minutes because they had been coming out of detention or whatever. And that made me want to come to work. Because I knew that these boys were smart. I would pull out my notebook and I would teach them some of the stuff I was learning because it had to do with what they were learning. And they would know it. And I knew they were smart and I knew they tried and they understood it. And I knew they were also the bad kids or whatever.

But then I'd be like, "I'm going to call your parents." And they would get themselves together. Or, "I've got a dollar for the first one to get this question right." And they would get themselves together.

So even though it was difficult kids, you just have to keep asking questions. "So what's x in this line?" And when I was asking them, "Where'd you get this answer? How did you get to that answer?"

Treat them like you care—I would give them hugs and tell them I'd see them tomorrow, at the end of each session. After I treated them like I care, they'd start caring. And they wanted to come back.

MODERATOR: But hold them to high standards.

CHANNELL: Challenge them. You've got to challenge them, because if you don't challenge them, they're not going to challenge themselves. And no one around them is going to challenge them.

MODERATOR: What changes do you see? Was there a change in how they behaved?

CHANNELL: Not only do they score high on their MSA [Maryland School Assessment] but first I was calling their parents, then they were calling me. First they were calling to say, "Please talk to his teacher, because he's not doing so well." Then it's, "He's doing so well that maybe you can go to his teacher and tell her how he's doing." It was to the point where I was meeting with their teachers, meeting with their parents, meeting with their friends who wanted to come in. They weren't getting in trouble. Their friends were coming. I want to see them in about five years.

CHANNELL: And to be teaching these Black boys, it just felt so good. And they live around here, where I don't want to say [it's] bad or whatever but it's not beautiful.

MICHELE: Establishing the relationship is really just working with them every day. You learn about them just in the few minutes before and after tutoring. The relationship just has to be there for it to work. And it kind of goes back to the conditions of the city schools. If you have thirty kids in class and one teacher, a teacher is not going to possibly be able to build a relationship. And that's one thing that we have that isn't in the schools the Algebra Project offers that.

CHELSEA: When I was in middle school, I only talked to people in my circle. If you weren't in my circle, I didn't talk to you. But now being out of high school and everything and being in the project for so long, I'll talk to strangers. I won't know you, but I'll start a conversation with you and become your friend.

CHRIS: I changed a lot in the tenth grade. That's when I really became a part of advocacy. And since then it's like you know, I'm talking and really open to people—smiling and all that, because I remember when I wouldn't even participate in class. Now they have me on radio shows and all that. Yeah, it's just really, really fun, yeah.

MODERATOR: You both said you've become more outgoing, more open, more self-confident? Say something about how.

CHRIS: You get a lot of compliments. It's like here, everybody knows you can do what you say you're going to do. And that's different in a lot of other places. And in school people expect you to do things not so well. Everybody here's positive—positive leaders and you get things done.

CHELSEA: I became more outgoing and charismatic, I guess, and good at public speaking. I was being thrown again [by Mr. Jay] into like going to school board meetings. Like, "Chelsea, you should go to the school board meetings. Has anybody told you she's speaking at the school board meeting? Chelsea, you should organize the next rally." And it got me involved.

RYAN: How it changed me? I always liked talking, being in the forefront. I never really liked following people. So it just really put me on another platform in front of my peers. I never really took a political standpoint. I mean I was in student government but that's not really politics. You know, if I was known for anything, it'd be for running my mouth. But it's for a positive reason, and people see that. And people give me my accolades for that because I'm running my mouth for the right reasons.

XZAVIER: I used to be crying just being an observer. Now you know, I worked with the Algebra Project, done so much work, that people out of nowhere are seeing me on TV. And I'll just be standing, and I'll notice some scary-looking dude, you know? With weapons on him that's visible so you have to see. He'll be like, "Hey, I saw you on TV. What you doing on TV for?" I would address them like, "Yeah, I was on TV" for this type of thing, you know. And now, when I'm around, like, a bunch of negative people, I can just come out and, "You know, what, blood? You know what we should be doing? You should really think about our community and see what we could do. You know what I'm saying? There's a whole bunch of us. We should think about how much work we could do out here besides robbing people and this and that."

MODERATOR: When they see you, how do they respond?

XZAVIER: They respond like, "You know what, we should, because I don't want to go back to jail." That's what they tell me: "I don't want to go back to jail. I know I could do better. I don't want to be harassed by the police every five seconds. I want to see how to make some legal money, some positive money." That's how they respond to me. Also it made me change my confidence. From the circumstances I was facing from what I saw from everyone else, going to college—it's one of my goals now, and I'm working real hard to get into college.

MICHELE: How the project has changed me? Prior to the Algebra Project I always knew I wanted to teach. But when I was getting into high school I was beginning to get discouraged because people would say, "You? You're so shy and nobody's going to listen to you." And I was really getting discouraged. I was observing the teachers that I was in class with, and I was saying, "Well, if my peers don't listen to them, what would make them listen to me?" And I was really struggling with that. But then when I joined the Algebra Project, and I started working with the clients and started tutoring them, I realized there's no way I can pass this up. I can't imagine not working with someone and seeing that lightbulb click in and say, I get it. I can't imagine not doing that.

Learning different strategies, [for] how to deal with troubled clients or things like that, it just really helped me stay focused and really helped me to know that I can do this.

CHARNELL: I was thinking about the conversation we had yesterday we were reading from Dr. Robert Moses's book, *Radical Equations*. And this is a book that we read like throughout the summers with the Algebra Project. But there was one part—somebody made the comment that they realized their worth in terms of the fight because they realized that they were citizens, and that they deserved everything that they were being denied. They realized their worth, in other words. After everything that they had been through, and they being us, our ancestors—they still were able to realize their worth, after posttraumatic slavery syndrome and all that.

And I always thought I had the idea of freedom. But I think when I came to the Algebra Project . . . it really started getting reshaped. And me and my best friend were the only two people from our 'hood that went to school outside of our neighborhood. Everybody else went to the zone school. And that one comment when the girl was like, "I didn't know you danced. I didn't know you wrote poetry. I didn't know you did this." And it just really dawned on me that I wasn't recognizing my own worth, which was limiting my freedom. But now I can just confidently say, "Oh, I work at the Algebra Project. I'm on the dean's list." And I feel okay about that. But expressing all the things that I had kept bottled up in my poetry journal for so long and coming out I think has a lot to do with the project.

MODERATOR: So how did it help you?

CHARNELL: This was one of the few environments where it was unacceptable to be sub par. In some environments it is acceptable to be sub par. Or I would notice people even in speech. I would notice students correcting students. And then we would hear people talk. "Okay, Chelsea, you did this well, you did this well. But you need to improve on this. Charnell, you did this well, you did this well, but you need to improve on that." So it's twofold. It's like you're expected to do excellent and above that but also people are going to help you to do better. They give you suggestions.

CHARNELL: Another thing that we had was the report card charts that we would check to see how people were doing in school, because—

MODERATOR: You tutors would check your client's report card?

CHARNELL: No. We tutors would check the tutors. Because again, it's all students. There was no adult checking us.

MODERATOR: So, accountability to one another.

CHARNELL: Exactly.

MODERATOR: What are the disadvantages of being a part of a student-run organization? I mean I've heard the advantages.

CHELSEA: I guess that there's an advantage and a disadvantage at the same time. You don't want to leave. Like you stay there throughout your whole high school career and then you go to college. But then you find your way to get back, because you don't want to leave. It's such a relaxed atmosphere that you get kind of comfortable with it and you use it like a crutch. You want to be involved as long as possible.

Another disadvantage is the fact that a lot of people don't even think that we're student-run. Like, they think that Mr. Jay and Mr. Nik tell us what to do, and that we're like their pawns or something. It's hard to not be part of that perception because they think that young people can't be independent.

MODERATOR: People don't think that young people care about education.

CHELSEA: Right. They say that we don't care about our education. They just think that we're programmed to what other people tell us to do. And it's definitely not the case here. We do everything. Mr. Jay and Mr. Nik are our advisors. They're here to help us when we need their help, and with, also, the legality issues. So, I mean, we do everything.

MICHELE: Another minor disadvantage is that at our sites we have site leaders and tutors. But the tutors, a lot of times, feel like they don't want to be responsible to someone who is their age or might be even younger than them.

CHARNELL: Another problem that we have is sometimes people

[not] taking us seriously. Like when we go to the board meetings and such. Or a good example is, recently when we were in court and I think they didn't want us to speak until Jill Carter, the delegate of the Forty-third District, got there. And one of us stepped up and said, "No, we represent ourselves." And I mean respectfully but once we present ourselves, a lot of times they do take us seriously. But their first instinct is, there's got to be some adult there that represents us.

CHARNELL: I was going to say the obvious issues that we already have to deal with is, [as] mostly Black, or of color, Baltimore City public school students. There's already an assumption. Just the racism and the attitudes toward us is already negative.

I've never seen so many police officers until we would have our rallies and our events. But when we had the mock trial [in] May of 2005 in commemoration of *Brown v. Board [of Education]*. Although schools are integrated, they're still very segregated: segregated in funds, segregated by resources.

And we were trying to change that through this demonstration. We had an open mic at the beginning by the harbor. And the idea was to, like, stop traffic in the busiest time of the day. So it was really cool because students were using every mechanism that they use— hip hop, poetry. X and Chris and Wayne's group, Militant Advocates, which is our hip hop group from the Algebra Project, they were spitting or rapping like poets, were doing their thing. And also the press was there.

And then we had the march from the harbor to the state school board, and as we were marching, we had a lot of different chants. And when we got to right across the street from the school board, we had this mock trial where I was the judge and Chris was a witness.

We wanted Nancy Grasmick and Governor Ehrlich to be on trial and to be tried just like . . . I mean, if I stole eight million dollars, there would be no question about being on trial. We did the trial and it was really powerful on a lot of different levels. And at the end of our trial, the order from Judge Covert, or myself, was that we would paste up these wanted signs, just like if someone had a warrant for their arrest.

As the students were crossing the street, posting up the flyers, the police officers weren't even giving them contact. There's no rule that says you can't post up flyers. But they were just ripping them down.

I've seen and I've been to antiwar protests where it's majority White, college students. I've been to stop apartheid and Rwanda protests. I've been to all different types of protests and never before have I seen the type of disrespect and blatant racism displayed through Baltimore City Police, except when it's the Baltimore Algebra Project and Black Baltimore City public school students. I know that that makes a difference.

I have to say for myself it was very difficult. It was very difficult to see my peers, and people that are my heroes, people that are making history. We have people coming in to talk to us about a book and what are you doing? You're not doing anything except harassing us.

CHRIS: I went to City College High School and it was very hard trying to spread the word throughout my school about what the Algebra Project's been doing. The teachers and the administrators were like against the Algebra Project. And I remember a couple years ago, the school was actually for it. You know, some of the same people that was for it. You know, they were down with it when we had a walkout.

But the year that just passed, I remember trying to get up on the intercom to advertise a conference we were having. A youth open mic, youth conference, and a party. And they would always ask me, "All right, is there a teacher that's sponsoring it?" I'm like, "No, it's the Algebra Project." "Well, you need an adult to do it."

There's like a lot of resistance inside of the schools, when we're really trying to help the schools out. And the teachers and administrators should understand that, but they're like with the school board's side for some reason.

CHRIS: Walkouts and strikes. Teachers were told to give, like, major tests during that day. And I remember we had a three-day strike. And I went on strike. But the thing is, a lot of students don't understand that it's power in numbers. We hold the power at the school. So I went on strike and I missed the test she was putting out. The teacher let me make it up, but my grades just bent a little bit. But the thing is, if all of us, you know, didn't come to that class . . .

MODERATOR: She couldn't fail everybody.

CHRIS: Right.

MODERATOR: How do other students react to you? How do students react to you as representatives [of] the Algebra Project, as representatives of a different something?

CHRIS: It varies. In school I do a lot of presentations. People, they'd be paying attention sometimes, though, but after a while they'd be like, "Ah, here we go with Chris again, about to talk about saving the world or some stuff." And then sometimes, you know, a lot of people would get interested and talk to me about it and how to join and all that.

FERNANDES: My school was very helpful as far as [the] Algebra Project. My school is New Era Academy, and we are a brand-new school. And when we were getting organized for the strikes and stuff, it's like the students in my school already knew me as being the radical person, kind of always standing up for other people. So when it was time to get organized for the strike I was in early in the morning, first person there, posting up flyers. And my principal asked me a couple questions in the hallway.

I'm like, "Remember the Baltimore Algebra Project?" He's like, "Baltimore Algebra Project?" And then I would sit down and explain to him. The principal was like my peer. I mean, even though he was very much older than I was, but he was very curious. He wanted to know.

We don't have an intercom in our school yet. So we usually just line up in the hallway. And that goes to the ninth, tenth, eleventh, and now that we have seniors; I will be in the first senior class. We're in the hallway and I can announce this to the whole entire school. I'll be, like, "We're having a strike." Or, "We're going to have this conference." And everybody's very much informed. And everybody likes me in school, especially the teachers.

But everybody in my school came to that school to work, because, you know, we're in uniform and tie. Much of the youth now don't want to go to school wearing a pair of slacks; dress shoes, shiny; a tie, buttoned. Everybody came there because they knew they were going to come there and get an education. They were going to leave from New Era Academy to go to college. And so everyone there was like we're ready. We're going to strike.

CHELSEA: For my first few years I went to City College. And that's when I first started getting involved in advocacy within the Algebra Project. And it was kind of hard to get people out because they thought that they had everything. They were like, "Well, we're fine. Our alumni [help] us out. We need this, we need that, then we've got it." But I had to make the point that, "Okay, well, that's being selfish."

"You obviously don't have everything. You go to Harford County, you go to Montgomery County, see what they have. Every student in their classroom has a laptop."

And then my last year I went to Heritage High School. That's in Lake Clifton now. And a lot of those students there just didn't care. They're like, "Well, I'm just here because I have to be, because I don't want my mother to go to jail, because I have to have a certain amount of attendance." And a lot of them were out there on the block dealing drugs and stuff like that. They're like, "It's not going to get any better. This is what we're going to get."

And I really wish I could take those people out to, a field trip to those richer counties in Maryland. And show them, "You deserve more. You deserve better. See what they get? And they're no different from you. So why shouldn't you receive the same thing?"

MODERATOR: And what do they say to you?

CHELSEA: They're just like, "I don't believe you." "It's not better anywhere else. Only the places where it's better is because they're White." And I'm like, "That's not necessarily true. You've got to believe in yourself and know that you deserve better." And they just didn't want to see that. But there're some people who are with me. Like, "Yeah I'm with you. I'm out there and we'll meet on the front lines."

Some people would agree about education and getting that and being good students and everything, but they didn't necessarily agree with our means. They didn't agree with maybe striking for three days. They're like, "Well, how is me missing school going to benefit me? I should be in school as much as I can. It might not be the best education but I should be in school getting that education."

But still, you're not going to get anything better unless you stand up for yourself, because no one else is standing up for you. A lot of the adults aren't standing up for you. Your parents are not standing up for you. So you have to do the work yourself. So it was a conflict of apathy and it was a conflict of the means to our end.

XZAVIER: I go around and try to express some knowledge with my peers. I'm not smarter than anybody but I just want to share something I learned today with someone else. I share some knowledge and a lot of times you know, some people would be, like, "Forget all that lame stuff. That stuff's for lames. That's not going to help me." Some people are offended by what I'm saying. Some people will be like, "You trying to say I'm dumb?" I'm like, "I ain't said nothing about that. I said you should fight for our education. Because they're giving us this education they found in the garbage, you know what I'm saying?"

MICHELE: On the issue of apathy, I actually think that Baltimore Polytechnic Institute is also one of the best schools in the city. And we also have a very good alumni association and giving money and stuff like that. And when the issue came up of strikes and rallies and things at the time, my senior year, we had an interim principal. And she made an announcement to everybody, saying, "Well, you have what you need. This is not a concern for you."

We had so many people telling us we should not be concerned with this because we had what we need. And so the adults basically looked down on us, trying to say that we were handling more than we should have been handling. And that it wasn't our role. It wasn't our place to do it.

MODERATOR: Students said the same thing?

MICHELE: Students began to agree with them. And as far as my peers, how they saw me as being in the Algebra Project, it wasn't a big thing.

WAYNE: I can honestly say at Heritage High School, I did not know one teacher that wasn't for the Algebra Project. And that's from us talking to them about it. But on the students' side, it wasn't a lot that was with us.

CHARNELL: My family was very supportive, because all my family is very active in terms of change. My grandmother was like kind of involved with Black Panthers. She was a nurse in a time when Black women weren't nurses. My grandfather was a Mason. So it's always been like this idea of change. My mother was very much involved and very outspoken. So I was always taught to speak out. I really didn't have enemies at school so I used that to my advantage.

MODERATOR: You're reminding me of something: that everybody has something they can contribute to change. The organizer's job is to figure out how to make that possible. The last sort of big area I wanted to talk about is all these activities you folks have done: the marches, rallies, et cetera. Of all the various tactics, events, actions that you've tried, which ones do you think have been the most effective? And then how did you pull it off?

CHELSEA: The most effective, I guess, means to an end that we've done is the most radical ones in my opinion. Because like when we tried to arrest Nancy Grasmick. We got targeted media attention from that. People would still identify us with that. "Oh, you tried to arrest the state superintendent? What are you guys? Who do you guys think you are?" Also, like, when we did a sit-in, in Bonnie Copeland's office, that was the previous CEO of Baltimore City public schools, we had a sit-in to meet with her. And she didn't meet with us. We had a rally outside, of supporters. The next day, she met with us and we told her what we wanted her to do.

For the sit-in, there were about five of us. And we went upstairs into her office and we asked, "Could we meet with Bonnie Copeland?" The security guard at the front desk was like, "Well, she's in a meeting." So we're like, "Okay, we'll wait for her until she gets out." And he's like, "Well she's going to be in meetings all day." Previously, we had scheduled a meeting with her on that day. So it's not like we just popped up out of nowhere. We tried to schedule this ahead of time.

So we said, "We'll wait for her." So we all sat down. And then, like, five minutes later school police came upstairs and they started arresting us one by one and took us downstairs to the basement. They tried all types of intimidation. For example, they had Chris all by himself outside while the rest of us were inside. They were cursing at us, telling us we were dumb. They separated us. They were trying to browbeat us. They were just being really nasty to us. And one guy told Charnell, well, like, "Well, yeah I've been in the movement. I marched with Martin Luther King." But we were stupid for doing what we were doing.

We met with Bonnie Copeland the next day. We told her that we wanted her to ask Nancy Grasmick, the state superintendent, for the money that we deserved. And we had made particular demands about our deficiency appropriation, which comes from the rainy day fund. And we asked could we have the one hundred ten million dollars deficiency appropriation from the state.

And then also our strikes for the three days this year—that's the longest we ever had a strike. We usually had a strike for a day. So that was monumental. And it was very radical. And as a result we had tons of media attention. We got tons of more allies, and as a result we were building on our demand.

Oh, yeah, we met with the mayor. The mayor actually wanted to meet with us. We didn't even set that up. He didn't agree to all of our points, [but] we weren't going to negotiate our stance. And obviously he didn't agree with all of them, so we took it that you don't agree at all. So we told that to the press.

CHANNELL: I just want to point out that one of the things that he did agree with was something that he didn't agree with last year, which was that the State did owe us money.

MODERATOR: So just getting that admission was a big step forward.

CHELSEA: Right. It's a step forward. We changed his mindset as far as the availability of money and the dire need for it. So he agreed that we needed this money and that we weren't receiving it. And that was just a political tactic because he's running for governor this year. But as the most effective means to an end, our most radical rallies have gotten us the best result.

CHARNELL: I think that the most effective thing was the first "Arrest Nancy Grasmick" moment on October twenty-sixth, 2004. This was our first time trying to arrest Nancy Grasmick. It was so powerful because we had a row of students from the Algebra Project as well as teachers. There was a little sitting area during these meetings. That whole sitting area was us. And we had signs that said like, "We want our one hundred and ten million dollars' deficiency appropriation," so on and so forth.

The first person to speak was Lorne and his first line was, "You political prostitutes." And that just like set off the whole climate. It made people very uncomfortable in terms of the school board. But it made the students very excited because I remember Lorne and myself taking so much time writing these speeches and thinking about what we were going to say.

It was on point. He went through everything in terms of what was owed. He went through, "How could you sleep at night when you have the blood of these many children that dropped out of school"—he was talking about the attrition rate—"on your hands?" It was just amazing.

And what was also amazing was that as soon as we started speaking, the people on the inside stood up silently and held their signs up. So the press could see that. And then he called for the arrest first. Then, Cheree came up and spoke her piece, which was also very powerful. And she called for the arrest. And the students were still standing up. The rally was still going on outside. And then I spoke. At this point they were not willing to hear anything that was really being said, I don't think.

I said, "Hello Nancy Grasmick. This speech is directed toward you." And she was crying. But I saw this as a defense mechanism, and I really didn't care if she was crying. I'd been crying. We've been crying. You can cry all you want. You're a grown woman. Get over it.

But she was crying about it, and I just kept talking. A lot of my speech was based around history. I was relating these times to slavery and calling Nancy Grasmick and her people new-age slave masters. And the people who weren't White and couldn't see themselves as slave masters were Uncle Toms. There was just a whole slew of emotion, but very valid.

As I was speaking, before I even got to that point they began to walk out. And I kept giving the speech. All of this was on tape. First they turned down my mic, so I didn't have a mic. So I was going to speak anyway. And everybody was supporting and screaming.

I was pushing through to get this speech out because I knew it had a purpose. My part was the last part to finalize the arrest, and turning to the trooper to arrest her, and the trooper was laughing. He wasn't listening.

So the reason I thought that was the most powerful because it may not seem the most successful was all the adversity that we had that day. I can't even explain the type of a feeling that we had speaking at that point, because we knew that we were taking a risk. I didn't know if I would be suspended. I was kind of expecting to get kicked out of City. They said they would arrest me if I kept talking. So I kept talking.

But I, everybody stuck together and really, really supported, and nobody said this is too radical. The reason why this is so significant is because this was at the point where they were planning on laying off about three hundred teachers. So the radicalness of that moment, and that whole atmosphere was crucial into leading up to everything else that we did.

As a result of this event, one, Nancy Grasmick actually did say that she was going to have a meeting with us, and she did. This was amazing to us because she hadn't done so up to this point. The meeting didn't really change much. We still presented the same things. She said she understood where we were coming from but we hurt her feelings. And we said, "We understand we hurt your feelings, but this isn't about your feelings. It's about the students, and for that, we don't apologize. We hope you feel better, but let's work through this." And she didn't want to.

But the good thing was that a lot of the teachers were not laid off as a result. There was a lot of press.

CHELSEA: We were just so monumental in the year 2004. We had the largest rally in 2004. We had over six hundred students and teachers and protesters outside of the state school board demanding a quality education. People were so angry and fed up. They were losing their counselor, they were losing their teachers, and they would lose some principals. All kinds of people throughout the city had the same problem and we all could connect with each other because we were all going through the same thing. We had tons of press. We were really central in this whole endeavor for adequate education. And I think it's important all around, but I think it's especially in Baltimore City because Baltimore City is one of the most dangerous cities in America, and we have one of the worst school systems in America. We've been put down so much as a city that it was really important to us to be involved and uplift our community than to add another bad statistic to our city.

MODERATOR: What's been the most effective and why? From which of these actions have you learned the most?

RYAN: I haven't been with the Algebra Project officially except for the last few months. But I think that each action that I have participated in has helped and contributed to our overall goal—from back when Charnell and the first people were in the state school board meeting down to the last time we were down there, because it shows consistency.

People look at things like the Million Man March, which happened ten years or eleven years ago. And people still say, "I was there. I went and I was counted." But the entire message of the Million Man March was, let's do something. We can all come together, now let's do something. But people went, they said rah, rah, rah, and everybody was there. I was there. And then come back home to these same conditions.

But the consistency of the Algebra Project before I was here, before everybody around this table had actually stepped into it, has been consistently growing, moving, and changing the mindsets of young people.

And so we keep on going even if we can't change the mindset of the adults, the hard-headed, stiff-necked, and rebellious adults. We may not be able to change them, but we have people like sister Charnell who are in college, going up the totem pole, and we keep recruiting more people, changing the mindsets while they're young. We can start an entire culture shift, like we were talking about in the meeting: demanding of our peers, the greater society, and ourselves. That's the three-tiered demand.

MODERATOR: Can you explain that?

RYAN: The three-tiered demand: appreciate the demands on yourself, so do what you need to do. The second demand is demand on your peers, so set an example through yourself to demand that they do something. The third demand is the demand on the larger society; demand everything that's around you to make a change. Those are the three-tiered demands. I learned that from the Baltimore Algebra Project.

WAYNE: I honestly believe that every event that we've done was effective, because every event had a new face, new media, and a new ally. That's what made us grow. That's what made us known in Baltimore City. So to me I believe every event, everything had an impact.

MICHELE: To add to what Wayne said, I was thinking that just our persistence makes it effective. The fact that we're doing one thing after another after another, at this point it almost doesn't matter [that it's] any particular event. It's just the fact that we're still out there pressuring these people no matter what type. Whether it's a sit-in, whether it's a march, whether it's a teacher, it just seems like as long as we're persistent with it, we get some type of effect.

MODERATOR: I grew up in the sixties. I think I over-value tactics. But when I went to Mississippi to interview folks about what they had done, it's persistence, persistence, persistence; not that you're doing different things but that you do the thing you're doing until you get a response. It's not that you have better ideas or just smarter tactics than anybody else. But you persist more.

CHARNELL: Well, one of my favorite quotes is from MLK is that "injustice anywhere is a threat to justice everywhere." So I think when we started expanding more in terms of just thinking bigger in terms of our results, and also anticipating answers. So for example, when we first started organizing, we may plan one event and just hope that they would say what we wanted them to say. But then as we grew, we realized that they weren't going to say what we wanted them say, so we would plan two events.

For example, we [would] begin the planning and know that we were going to have a follow up on this day. I couldn't really answer the question about which one is most effective, because each event led up to the next event. And the next event led up to the last event. And the last event can always go back to the first. So it all seems to be interconnected to me. If the first "arrest Nancy Grasmick" wasn't there then it would have been later on that we decided on that.

And I think also that we really started to ask the questions that we may have seen as redundant as first. Early on we didn't really ask as many questions like, what is it that we want to keep saying? Because we knew what we wanted, but we got very precise. We would keep repeating. The media would ask us our name and we would say, "We want the one hundred ten million dollar deficiency appropriation." And they would say well what school do you go to? "We want the one hundred ten million dollar deficiency appropriation."

But then on another level, we were also listening. We would take suggestions from rallies and protests and sit-ins, and see what students thought could be improved on, because those are the people we want to be there. We started asking what they want. Well, I want to listen to some music while we're there. Well, okay, is there a way we can incorporate that? I know that [Ryan's] rap group made a club mix—club music is really big here with the youth—for one of our new slogans, "No education, no life." And mad people would just listen to it and, like, oh, I like that club mix. Well you played it and everybody was like, oh, this is hot. . . . Just really building our own culture, because then people will come.

It's been a lot more successful because we were listening, which is one thing that most adults don't do. They don't listen. So we were listening to everything that people were saying to us. Even the things that we didn't think were true. And we took the things that we saw as relevant and used them. And still kept the message the same.

For additional information about the Baltimore Algebra Project, go to www.baltimore-algebra-project.org.

NOTES

1. Ella Baker, "The Challenge of the Age and the Negro Youth," n.d., Ella Baker Papers, box 1, folder 2, Schomburg Center for Research in the Black Culture.
2. Florence Howe, "Mississippi's Freedom Schools," in *Myths of Coeducation: Selected Essays* (Bloomington: Indiana University Press, 1984), 9.
3. Charles M. Payne, "Introduction," in *Teach Freedom: Education for Liberation in the African-American Tradition*, eds. Charles M. Payne and Carol Sills Strickland (New York: Teachers College Press, 2008), 5–6.
4. Casey Hayden, "Ella Baker as I Knew Her: She Trusted Youth!" *Social Policy* 34, no. 2 (2003): 101.

PART II

Can the Constitution Guarantee Quality Education?

2

Reading, Writing, and Rights

Ruminations on Getting the Law
in Line with Educational Justice

Imani Perry

I was sitting in front of a classroom of law students. The room was beautiful in a manner rarely found outside the most affluent institutions, bright, new and comfortable and yet bestowed with the elegant features of an old and stately place. We were in the middle of a semester in which we were studying the critical race theory movement in legal scholarship. This movement, which began with a few renegade law students and professors, has rejected color-blind constitutionalism and instead uses race consciousness to explore how the law continues to support and extend racial inequality.[1] It is a movement of critical deconstruction, pursued with the goal of advocating for racial justice in light of the realities of a post–de-jure-segregation society. I have taught this movement as an academic subject for four years now and am continually pleased at how many law students, who are so often stereotyped as selfish and self-interested, are engaged by the subject.

This particular group of students, whom I taught while on a semester-long visit away from my home institution, had proven to be an intelligent, impassioned, and creative group, so I eagerly presented the question for the day.

"Given that there is such a great deal of inequality in education, and that the inequality is both race- and class-based, how would you, as future attorneys, fashion an argument for quality education as a right?" The silence of thirty seconds was followed by a student stating, with furrowed brow, "There is no such right. The Court has already decided that issue." I looked around the classroom, and other heads bobbed up and down affirming that, yes, she had gotten the question right. I prodded, then pushed for a few moments, but they wouldn't budge. The question had been answered.

In a law school context, indeed, the student had gotten the question right. In *San Antonio School District v. Rodriguez*, 411 U.S.31.1. (1973), the United States Supreme Court stated that public education is not a right granted to individuals by the Constitution. The Supreme Court has asserted that there is no constitutional right to education at all, much less equal or quality education. However, the Court has also acknowledged that education is not "merely some government benefit indistinguishable from other forms of social welfare legislation. Both the importance of education in maintaining our basic institutions, and the lasting impact of its deprivation on the life of the child, mark the distinction."[2] It is indeed integral to the very fabric of our democracy.

However, beginning as early as the noncommittal "all deliberate speed" mandate in Brown II, it has become clear that the federal judiciary has consistently, even doggedly, failed to support equality goals in American education, even while acknowledging how fundamental education is to the fabric of our society. The fight for equal education in the post-*Brown* era seems to the American law student a dead end.

But many of the most important constitutional provisions have been those which have emerged after appearing to be dead ends. The Thirteenth, Fourteenth, and Fifteenth amendments, guaranteeing freedom, citizenship, and suffrage rights to African Americans, were ratified only a decade after the Dred Scott decision, in which the Supreme Court invalidated congressional authority to limit slaveholding in the territories by sustaining the enslavement of a Black man and wife who had been taken to a free area. What is clear is that activism and public will are critical to constitutional re-interpretation of the sort that would be required to affirm a right to a quality education.

In order for the constitutional right to a quality education to be recognized, it would have to be established that, one, education is indeed a right, and, two, there are standards necessary in order for a citizen or resident to exercise that right in a meaningful fashion.

Scholars have been struggling with the challenges at the intersection of race, law, and education for a number of years. One such scholar, Derrick Bell, has been a leading critic of the manner in which lawyers pursuing law to advance racial justice have often put their ideological goals before the interests of their clients. According to Bell, the emphasis on integration in *Brown* and the cases which followed it, rather than quality or resources, was evidence of this misapplication of energy.[3] But it is not merely ideology that often impedes legal thinkers when imagining their role in resolving social problems. It is precedent, both in the technical sense, i.e. the rules that have already been established in the law, and in the figurative sense, methods of thinking about what law can do based upon what law has done.

It is without question that pursuing the goal of recognizing that there is a constitutional right to quality education requires thought that lies against the grain in many ways. One conceptual barrier may be the tradition of the legal branch of the civil rights struggle. Historically, African Americans have struggled for and won their rights through making arguments about the denial of their substantive federal constitutional rights—rights that are explicitly guaranteed in the Constitution yet have been denied by states or their agents.

Because there is no such guaranteed federal right to education, many have argued that we should understand that inadequate and unequal education is in violation of equality provisions of the Constitution, specifically as they protect the rights of racial minorities. While there is no question that the inequality of education offers clear evidence of how states sustain racial inequality, even if doing so is unintentional, getting from there to a cognizable, or, better stated, recognized, denial of equal protection rights on the basis of racial discrimination has been, as yet, an impossible journey.

There appear to be several alternative potential lines of argument. One, which has proven successful before some state courts, has been to argue for the right to a quality or equal education under state constitutions. Education has always been the province of the states. Local governance of education, despite its association with historic and ongoing racial inequality, does have some benefits, particularly with respect to community control of educational institutions and the possibilities for sophisticated evaluation of educational programs, as well as experimentation. Setting aside for the moment reported problems with implementation and avoidance, the *Abbott v. Burke* decisions, in which the New Jersey State Supreme Court mandated equalized funding and minimum standards in order to remedy a violation of state guarantees of equal protection, signify an important move of courts to a more sophisticated analysis of what constitutes inequality in the contemporary United States. There has been a range of subsequent *Abbott* opinions, the latest in 1998. In sum, the *Abbott* educational adequacy opinion included the following elements:

- "Rigorous content standards-based education, supported by per-pupil funding equal to spending in successful suburban schools
- "Universal, well-planned and high quality preschool education for all three- and four-year olds
- "Supplemental ("at-risk") programs to address student and school needs attributed to high-poverty, including intensive early literacy, small class size and social and health services
- "New and rehabilitated facilities to adequately house all programs, relieve overcrowding, and eliminate health and safety violations
- "School and district reforms to improve curriculum and instruction, and for effective and efficient use of funds to enable students to achieve state standards
- "State accountability for effective and timely implementation, and to ensure progress in improving student achievement"[4]

Legal scholar Goodwin Liu has proposed another legal strategy, which is to argue that the current educational inequality between states, in which those states with high proportions of people of color spend less on education and are less effective according to a number of measures, amounts to a violation of equal protection that should be actionable. He asserts that "existing interstate disparities in educational opportunity stand in tension with the Fourteenth Amendment guarantee of national citizenship and that ameliorating the disparities is a constitutional duty of the federal government."[5] Presumably, if the Supreme Court were willing to mandate the equalization of funding between states or uphold a congressional act doing so, that opinion would then facilitate work within states to equalize funding, resources, or otherwise remedy the inevitable ongoing intrastate, even intra-district racial disparities. Hence, there is an implicit two-pronged strategy that would follow from Liu's proposals, with the federal preceding the state-based one.

Constitutional theorist Alexander Tsesis argues that the Thirteenth Amendment provides a means for addressing educational inequality along the lines of race.[6] The text of the Thirteenth Amendment is

> Section 1. Neither slavery nor involuntary servitude, except as a punishment for crime where of the party shall have been duly convicted, shall exist within the United States, or any place subject to their jurisdiction.
> Section 2. Congress shall have the power to enforce this article by appropriate legislation.

The second section allows for a legislative response to the "badges and incidents" of servitude which the Supreme Court included as attendant to the prohibition upon slavery in its early Thirteenth Amendment cases. Although most later Supreme Court cases have failed to interpret violations of the Thirteenth Amendment to include anything but literal enslavement, if Congress were to enact legislation intended to address the badges and incidents of servitude, the Court presumably would have to allow it.

There is a relatively straightforward argument that the minimal access to quality education available to African American students is a result of the "badges and incidents" of slavery. Through the first half of the twentieth century, African Americans were systematically excluded from purchasing property in what were or would become affluent areas (and good school districts) by the proliferation of racially restrictive covenants that prevented home owners from selling to African Americans, as well as extralegal violence when African Americans attempted to integrate predominantly White neighborhoods all over the country. At the same time, the postwar Federal Housing Authority Underwriters manuals that directed mortgage lenders to assess lower values for homes in African American neighborhoods and the practice of redlining ensured that African Americans would not see significant appreciation in home values over the course of the twentieth century. This directly undermined the property-tax base for funding schools in African American neighborhoods. The trickle-down effect of these practices in both private contracting and with governmental authority was White flight and disaccumulation in urban centers.

But we can also go back even further to find support for the argument that Congress should act to address the badges and incidents of servitude in education. The denial of education was a signature feature of enslavement in the United States. State legislation frequently made teaching a slave to read a criminal act. Unsurprisingly, along with property ownership and suffrage, literacy was one of the immediate desires of the formerly enslaved, and the multiracial Reconstruction governments therefore brought universal public education to the South. Access to education was immediately understood as a core element of freedom.[7] If we understand this, along with embracing the practical wisdom of conceiving of education as preparation for citizenship and civic membership, we should pressure Congress to act in the interests of our children and pursue legislation to address education. This legislation could be written so as to demand that states provide a quality education to all of their children. While redistributing funding is one means of doing so, Congress could encourage innovation on the part of states, and states could attempt a wide variety of means to substantially improve education. For example, states might provide increased income to master teachers and administrators who serve in areas of concentrated poverty, provide free professional development at state universities for educators who agree to serve in poor districts for a certain number of years, conceive of resource redistribution more broadly to include free access for children and families to cultural institutions like museums and theaters, with state-sponsored curricula attached to this access. Additionally, states could provide parents with home-based curricula, books, and materials as a supplement to school-based learning. There are obviously a plethora of possibilities, but the point is that it would be best for Congress to allow states to consider the goal of equity and quality with depth and nuance, inclusive of but not limited to basic economic factors.

Another possibility, one that has yet to appear to my knowledge in the legal literature, is to bring the Ninth Amendment to bear on arguments against racial inequality in education. The Ninth Amendment guarantees that the Court will not allow rights that exist but that are not enumerated in the Constitution to be denied. It is essentially a tool of interpretation, one that is very rarely successfully invoked. The signature expression of the Ninth Amendment is the right to an abortion, as acknowledged in *Roe v. Wade,* as an extension of privacy rights. We have nothing else, besides the privacy right, that we can point to in constitutional law as an explicitly protected unenumerated right.

But is also true that we have in constitutional law construed many provisions of the Constitution quite broadly in order to extend the arm of constitutional protection and rights. While overwhelmingly these things are not under the auspices of unenumerated rights, they at times effectively operate as such because they do not clearly (or even convincingly) flow from an enumerated right, and yet they seem to be "right" according to our law and culture. For example, I would argue that when the Court acknowledged workers' right to organize and collectively bargain, it became, effectively, an unenumerated right (albeit not invoked as such in case law).

Among legal scholars there is a conflict about how (and if) we should recognize unenumerated rights. While some have suggested that the framers only intended it to apply to the rights found in state constitutions at the time of its ratification, i.e., nothing more than an assurance of federalism, others have argued that such an interpretation lies contrary to the notion of a living constitution and renders the provision moot, given the guarantees of the Tenth Amendment. Randy Barnett, perhaps the foremost scholar in this area, has argued that we understand unenumerated rights as a kind of liberty interest. Barnett sees the Court's opinion in *Lawrence v. Texas* 539 U.S. 558 (2003), the case that struck down the Texas anti-sodomy statute that was previously upheld in *Bowers v. Hardwick* 478 U.S. 186 (1986), as a reinterpretation away from the privacy right asserted in *Roe* and its forerunners. Instead, according to Barnett, it was an acknowledgment of a liberty interest which he describes as "the properly defined exercise of freedom that does not violate the rights of others."

This notion of liberty interest is interesting and perhaps useful for advocates of equality beyond the realm of what occurs in a private domestic space so long as we understand it as also "freedom to," rather than merely "freedom from." While according to conventional wisdom one might see the liberty interest only as freedom from government intrusion into one's private places, we should also see it as freedom to participate fully in the body politic. Education is critical to civic participation and engagement, as the courts have consistently acknowledged, and to the expression of the full benefits of citizenship and residence in the nation state. That education would be systematically unequal along the lines of race (a form of inequality that is disallowed under enumerated rights) is untenable.

There are many in legal academia who would consider the foregoing paragraph as full of intentionally obfuscating rhetoric, arguing that replacing one little word to change "freedom from" to "freedom to," is far bigger than I let on. The former merely requires the government to leave people alone. It bespeaks the longstanding libertarian thread in our constitutional law and traditions, while the latter requires a significant infrastructural commitment of the sort not fully articulated in constitutional law until after the New Deal.

That may be, but it is, in this context, a commitment that is nothing more and nothing less than the realization of two commitments already made by our state and federal governments in law and policy —to school our citizens and to guarantee them racial equality and due process under the law.

The "freedom to" idea also calls into question the tension that has existed between liberty and equality, or equal protection and due process, in which efforts to ensure equality are often seen as invasive of individual rights, two interests that must be balanced. Instead, we should see that the very prospect of expressing individual rights effectively depends upon fair access, knowledge, and skills among our populations.

Under a conventional originalist interpretation, there is no question the framers would not have seen education, much less equal or quality education as a right—given that universal public education did not appear until the nineteenth century. However, it is clear that education was always highly correlated to notions of equal protection. Indeed, the common school movement appears as a result of the post–Civil War educational movements among African Americans and the work of the Freedman's Bureau. And it is also clear that for over a century we have understood education as a central part of our citizenship—with every state having mandatory education that reaches from early childhood into mid-adolescence.

In *Griswold v. Connecticut* 381 U.S. 479 (1965), the United States

Supreme Court overturned a state statute prohibiting contraceptives. In that case the Supreme Court stated that the right to privacy could be discerned in the emanations and penumbras of enumerated rights. I would argue that, given the history of Reconstruction and *Brown v. Board*, the right to education can be discerned in the emanations and penumbras of equal protection and due process. The Court's argument in *Griswold* was largely dependent upon earlier cases protecting freedom of association, *NAACP v. Alabama* 357 U.S.449 (1958) and *NAACP v. Burton* 371 U.S. 415 (1963). Importantly, these were civil rights cases in which the Court protected the rights of NAACP members to associate with each other privately. This case history demonstrates how interdependent ideals of liberty and the protection of equality actually can be. The liberties of NAACP members and their Black constituents could only be exercised if equality provisions were likewise protected.

The eminent early republic historian Bernard Bailyn has argued that Madison saw the Ninth Amendment as necessary because "in addition to the rights specified by the states, there is a universe of rights, possessed by the people—latent rights, still to be evoked and enacted into law."[8] Under such an interpretation of the amendment, alongside the history of the last one hundred years or so, it seems odd that education would not be seen as such a latent right. And, moreover, it seems wrong that it would not be seen as a civil right.

So you might wonder, if all of this is true, why do law students (and lawyers and law professors) believe that the fight for quality education as a constitutional right is a losing battle? To answer this, we must consider context.

Howard Zinn has written, "The Constitution, like the Bible, is infinitely flexible and is used to serve the political needs of the moment. . . . The law can be just; it can be unjust. It does not deserve to inherit the ultimate authority of the divine right of the king."[9] The decisions made in *Roe v. Wade* and the establishment of the National Labor Relations Board both occurred in the context of larger social justice movements. It was not an objective constitutionalism that led to those results, but a movement context. Zinn goes on to say in the same piece

> The Constitution gave no rights to working people: no right
> to work less than twelve hours a day, no right to a living wage,

no right to safe working conditions. Workers had to organize, go on strike, defy the law, the courts, the police, create a great movement which won the eight-hour day, and caused such commotion that Congress was forced to pass a minimum wage law, and Social Security, and unemployment insurance.

Zinn's point is that activism, not constitutionalism, has created so many of the legal protections we hold dear.

Now, it is not some crudely executed bunch of protests that create the mechanism whereby movement changes law. It is thoughtful activism and finding a path of argumentation in the context of movements. In this context we are being required to explore new paths in the twenty-first century. If we look to the legacy of social justice movements around race alone for our models, we find ourselves bound by trying to think in the context of enumerated federal rights, rather than state constitutional rights, Congressional legislation, or unenumerated rights. But looking at these other historic decisions is key to imagining how one might get to a different and more just conclusion about the nation's responsibility to educate children than what we currently have.

The first strike in the United States was that of the Philadelphia Printers of 1786, heralding a long history of protest on the part of workers. Over the years, the nation witnessed the sagas of the Molly Maguires, the Haymarket Riot, and the Pullman Strike. But it was the cumulative power of the labor movement in the early twentieth century, with the rapid expansion of the American Federation of Labor and the International Workers of the World, as well as cold war–incited fears of what disempowered yet organized workers would do in the wake of the Great Depression, that led to the passage of the National Labor Relations Act in 1935. In that act, the statement that "[t]he denial by employers of the right of employees to organize and the refusal by employers to accept the procedure of collective bargaining lead to strikes and other forms of industrial strife or unrest"[10] fundamentally changed the relationship between the law and workers. The test, however, was when the Supreme Court was asked to review the constitutionality of the act. When the Court affirmed the constitutionality of the act, it stated, "a single employee was helpless in dealing with an employer; that he was dependent ordinarily on his daily wage for the maintenance of himself and family; that if the employer refused to pay him the wages that he thought fair, he was nevertheless unable to leave the employ and resist arbitrary and unfair treatment; [and] that union was essential to give laborers opportunity to deal on an equality with their employer."[11] It was an acknowledgment of the injustice of the exploitation and manipulation of power on the part of employers, not merely a technocratic interpretation of law, that shaped judicial review.

The Court reached the conclusion it did under the national commerce power held by congress. The NLRB had found that the Jones and Laughlin Steel Corporation had engaged in unfair labor practices. And the Court allowed Congress to punish such practices because Congress has the authority to regulate interstate commerce, even if the actions in question were not directly related to interstate commerce. The idea was that unrest could lead to strikes, which could lead to lowered production, which would affect interstate commerce. So by upholding the legislation the Court effectively granted rights to employees that had not been enumerated or codified in the Constitution, in order to meet the demands issued by the labor movement.

Many things we take for granted, such as bargaining over wages, hours, health benefits, pensions, and sick days, all emerged out of the establishment of the NLRA and the NLRB. While the scope of employee rights under the act and board have diminished over the last several decades, it is critical to understand how essential most of these rules have become and how they directly emerged from a history of strikes and labor organizing done in a fashion that was, before the NLRA was passed, illegal. Even without an enumerated legal right, the Court did acknowledge the rights of employees in what I would call a sort of liberty interest that entailed both freedom *from* (prohibition, retribution, penalty for organizing) and freedom *to* (participate in institutions and political sphere in collective manner), vis-à-vis their employers. The Court sought to acknowledge and remedy the inequality of power in that instance by interpreting the Constitution to allow workers the right to use what power they had at their disposal, a collective power in numbers.

I reference this politico-legal history not because it is more compelling or inspiring than that of the civil rights movement or other social justice movements, but because it provides a context in which the law wasn't there until the people were. In the case of the civil rights movement, the constitutional provisions of the Thirteenth, Fourteenth, and Fifteenth Amendments had been so grossly misinterpreted that the legal argument, while very hard fought and carefully strategized, was clean and direct. In this case, it was less so. Nevertheless, a set of legal remedies emerged in response to the people.

Moreover, the exploration of the variety of histories in which social justice movements have led to legal change is important because we may begin to think of cases and how to use them in different ways. For example, the very case that was so essential to the road to civil rights and the maintenance of worker rights, *U.S. v. Carolene Products Co.*, 304 U.S. 144 (1938), because of its affirmation of the protection of the rights of "discrete and insular minorities" is a case which in some ways has limited the reach of the Ninth Amendment because it narrowed the scope of rights that may be protected by the courts and therefore could prove to be a significant challenge for the kind of argument suggested herein. That is merely to say that the cases seen as support for civil rights goals may instead be ambiguous as we look to new strategies of argument, and other cases not previously considered useful may suddenly become essential. We should be consistently exploring the legal and political history that is connected to social justice movements of various sorts. This is true even for those movements that may not appear to be as politically sympathetic to civil rights as the labor movement. For example, the grassroots networks that have defined the scope of the unenumerated right to privacy to include abortion have done so through political organizing that has led to legislative influence on the state level. There may be something useful to be found in that history as well.

Also, labor history is instructive because, like the civil rights movement, it led to remedies that emerged from legislation as well as judicial review. So imagine if, in coming years, the legislative branch were to decide, in response to social movement and public will, to institute equalizing educational reformation, we'd want the Supreme Court to acknowledge the right of Congress or a state legislature to do so because of a compelling state interest in education and equality. The congressional authority to engage in such an act could likely be construed from a number of provisions. But the point is that it would be important for the Court to be already inclined toward protecting such an act on the part of Congress, given that there would likely be a long litany of protests and claims against such an action, ranging from property rights (if school funding were no longer based on the property tax base) to states' rights arguments (if federal intervention were required by state education law). The dynamic interaction between legislatures and courts in reaching education goals is particularly salient if, as suggested here, an unenumerated rights argument were to become central to this movement. Even accepting the argument of noted constitutional scholar Laurence Tribe—"It is a common error, but an error nonetheless, to talk of 'Ninth Amendment rights.' The Ninth Amendment is not a source of rights as such; it is simply a rule about how to read the Constitution"[12]—the invocation of those rights in the context of quality education demands would still likely entail legislative impetus. That could simply mean that while an unenumerated rights claim would not mandate that states create a particular education structure, it would likely deem efforts to enforce equality via legislation constitutionally protected (and efforts to enforce inequality unconstitutional) because the Court would not deny the fundamental right to citizens.

The reason such an argument is rare among legal academics is not because it is so hard to reach or innovative, but because it lies far afield of what the standard rules of interpretation have become under constitutional law. The sensibility that provokes such unconventional argument is one that begins the analysis not with the law as it is, but with history and the goals of civil society. There are other potential lines of argument that may prove more or less fruitful and which also merit exploration. For example, a revisiting of the privileges and immunities clause of the Fourteenth Amendment, which was made impotent by the *Slaughter-house Cases* 83 U.S. 36 (1872), might be an alternative means of getting to a just educational system at law. Or we might turn completely to state constitutional law. The point here is not to argue aggressively for a particular argument but rather to provide one of many possible examples of exploring legal interpretation in the interest of the right to an education. Even though my students were wise enough not to jump into the challenging terrain of arguing against precedent, I hope that more of us can be courageous enough to do so. *Bowers v. Hardwick* was overturned in seventeen years; we've had over thirty since *San Antonio v. Rodriguez*.

Conventional wisdom has been that it was the opinion in *Brown v. Board of Education* 349 U.S. 294 (1954) that provided impetus to the civil rights movement. With the moral authority that comes from a Supreme Court opinion, African Americans could, for the first time in, depending on your math, sixty to seventy-five years, invoke the Constitution and have power behind that invocation in their struggles for social justice. Derrick Bell and Mary Dudziak have directed us, however, to look at what was happening politically that led the Court to make that decision. The Cold War, according to them, cast a damning light on American apartheid and demanded a reckoning by the highest court. But, too, it was the witness of the African American GI who fought fascism abroad in World War II only to return to de jure White supremacy at home. All of this is to say that we should not simply think of courts as facilitating social change but rather of social change facilitating good behavior on the part of courts.

The social justice work described in other chapters of this book, from that which is engaged in by students and communities to that which is done by teachers in classrooms, must be the vanguard of the move toward constitutional reinterpretation. Not only because courts are more likely to move in the same direction as engaged citizens, but also because that work changes our story about what citizens can expect, even demand, as citizens.

There is a tragic romanticism to the manner in which those of us in privileged spheres like law schools talk about inequality. We narratively juxtapose the book-lined walls, comfortable chairs, and letters of distinction following our names with the dank and desperate spheres of the less fortunate. In the midst of that self-congratulatory posture are debilitating intellectual blinders. Put another way, if one interprets what may be done only through the text and context of discourses among elites, one misses where the most important intellectual and moral transformations in our law have usually been born and nurtured. We did not get to the Thirteenth, Fourteenth, and Fifteenth Amendments through congressional debates alone—slave narratives, radical abolitionism, the Underground Railroad, the defection of slaves to Union lines during the Civil War all provided the groundwork.

As a law professor I am supposed to teach my students how to use the rule of law in order to make the best argument for their clients, or, if imagining themselves as future jurists, how to objectively interpret existing law. As a critical race theorist, I am charged with interpreting the law with the goal of racial justice in mind and even with making arguments as to what the law should be. But that work is without meaning if it is not connected to like arguments from communities. Lawyers who work in the public interest must be followers (or better yet, members) as much if not more than they are leaders.

I left the classroom on the aforementioned day despondent. I sadly thought, If bright young law students cannot imagine something different, or even some creative path toward getting to a better state of affairs, what hope do we have? But in retrospect that despondency was as disturbingly defeatist as their response to my question. Frederick Douglass famously said, "Power concedes nothing without a demand." We would all do well to heed that aphorism. Today, with sanitized images of the civil rights movement, which depict martyrdom without strategy, courage without intellect, and heroism without organization, we forget the complex processes that may be involved with issuing a demand. Douglass, who reinterpreted the Constitution from a slave-holding, property-fetishizing document to one through which he could argue for his rights as a Black American, understood that better than anyone. To state it simply, as Douglass and his political brethren would say, we cannot take "no" for an answer. It is my hope that this simple article might be a reminder that we must not think of law as either static nor disconnected from people, but rather as a tool for hewing the world into something more beautiful. A tool that must, itself, be hewn.

NOTES

1. For a good introduction to the field of critical race theory, see Kimberle Crenshaw et al., eds., *Critical Race Theory: The Key Writings That Formed the Movement* (New York: New Press, 1996).
2. *Plyler v. Doe* 457 U.S. 202 (1982).
3. See Derrick Bell, "Time for the Teachers: Putting Educators Back into the Brown Remedy," in *The Derrick Bell Reader*, eds. Richard Delgado and Jean Stefancic (New York: New York University Press, 2005), 226–31.
4. *Abbott v. Burke*. The Education Law Center, www.edlawcenter.org/ELC Public/AbbottvBurke/AboutAbbott.htm. Retrieved November 23, 2009.

5. Goodwin Liu, "Education, Equality, and National Citizenship," University of California at Berkeley Public Law Research Paper No. 832604, 1.

6. Alexander Tsesis, *The Thirteenth Amendment and American Freedom* (New York: New York University Press, 2004).

7. See Heather Andrea Williams, *Self-Taught: African American Education in Slavery and Freedom* (Chapel Hill: University of North Carolina Press, 2007).

8. Bernard Bailyn, "The Living Past—Commitments for the Future." Remarks to the White House Millennium Council, February 11, 1998.

9. Howard Zinn, "It's Not Up to the Court," *Progressive,* November 2005. Available at http://www.progressive.org/mag_zinn1105.

10. National Labor Relations Act, Section 1.

11. *NLRB v. Jones & Laughlin Steel Corp.,* 301 U.S. 1, 33 (1937).2.

12. See Laurence H. Tribe, *American Constitutional Law* 776, n. 14 (2nd ed. 1998).

3

Schools That Shock the Conscience

What *Williams v. California* Reveals
about the Struggle for an Education on
Equal Terms Fifty Years after *Brown*

Jeannie Oakes

More than two thousand young Latino and African American adolescents (32 percent of them still learning English; 77 percent poor) attend an urban California middle school that I call UCMS. These eleven- to fourteen-year-olds at UCMS spend three years crowded into a trash-littered space designed to hold four hundred fewer students; they are taught by inexperienced and untrained teachers who lack the books, equipment, and materials they need to teach. Let me tell you a bit more about it.

Only 43 percent of the teachers at UCMS are certified, and many teach outside their subject areas. One teacher assigned to a "sheltered" class for English learners said that she thought the class "was for foster care students from homeless shelters. I had never heard of sheltered." Long-term substitutes fill many positions for which teachers cannot be found at all. The school's day-to-day substitutes—many lacking subject-matter expertise or the ability to manage young adolescents—often let the students play or watch a movie instead of teaching.

UCMS students do all of their reading at school since there are not enough books for them to take home. English learners have nothing to read in their home languages. Science classrooms lack running water, lab tables, or equipment. Students have no calculators in math class, even though the state standards require middle school students to use them. Math manipulatives, such as counting blocks, are in short supply. Students sometimes spend a several minutes of instructional time in math class making their own graph paper. In some English classes, students can't look up misspelled words, definitions, or conduct any classroom research, because there are no dictionaries, thesauruses, or other reference materials. In social studies, many students make do without globes or other visuals, and they use atlases that are falling apart. One classroom does have a map, but only because an uncertified teacher's college supervisor "felt sorry" and gave her one.

Many UCMS teachers would like to photocopy materials for their students, often an option at schools in affluent neighborhoods. However, with at least 175 students per teacher, the school's limit of 150 photocopies a day for each teacher and 500 sheets of copy paper a month, it's not often possible. Besides, one of the school's two photocopying machines has been broken almost all year. Many teachers spend their own money at copy centers, as well as purchasing the books, manipulatives, and science supplies to teach standards-based lessons.

Because of the overcrowding, many teachers "rove" between classrooms, and some teach in spaces not intended to be classrooms at all, such as an upstairs gymnasium. One teacher said, "I have more kids than space. I have no room for anything other than sitting." A science teacher who wants students to do hands-on experiments complained that her classroom is too cramped. The heaters in some classrooms get so hot that students touching them are burned, but overcrowding has meant that teachers must put desks next to these heaters anyway. All 2,025 students eat lunch at once in an outside space with seating for only about five hundred students. Students say they often feel unsafe during the chaotic lunch period and that there is rarely time to get through the lunch line.

The school's water fountains are dirty, and many don't work at all. The school has no playground equipment, save several basketball hoops without nets. The bathrooms are covered with graffiti, and some teachers won't allow students to use the bathroom because "they get jumped" by students who cut classes, roam the school, and cause problems, including breaking second-story windows. The bathrooms opening out onto the schoolyard are considered unsafe because no one monitors them.

The gates surrounding the school have large gaps connected by chains, and patches cover large holes in the fences. Workmen drive their trucks onto campus and walk around without identification, and no one questions unidentified visitors as they enter and leave the campus. The building is unlocked only from 7:00 a.m. to 4:30 p.m. during the week and never on weekends. Unlike schools in affluent neighborhoods where committed teachers arrive early and work beyond the school day, both teachers and students at this school discouraged from doing either.

The students attending middle schools in nearby, mostly White, middle-class suburbs experience few, if any, of these problems.

The year is 2002—two years after the state was sued for forcing students to attend schools with substandard conditions.

LEGACIES OF *BROWN* AND *PLESSY*

In 1954, Chief Justice Earl Warren wrote for a unanimous Supreme Court in *Brown v. Board of Education:*

> In these days, it is doubtful that any child may reasonably be expected to succeed in life if he is denied the opportunity of an education. Such an opportunity, where the state has undertaken to provide it, is a right which must be made available to all on equal terms.[1]

The *Brown* case struck down the sixty-year-old *Plessy v. Ferguson* decision.

> The object of the [Fourteenth A]mendment was undoubtedly to enforce the absolute equality of the two races before the law, but in the nature of things it could not have been intended to abolish distinctions based upon color, or to enforce social, as distinguished from political equality, or a commingling of the two races upon terms unsatisfactory to either.[2]

In *Plessy,* the 1896 Court had ruled that legally enforced segregation did not violate the Constitution, as long as the separate facilities for Blacks were equal to those for Whites. Today, fifty years after *Brown,* the decision reversing *Plessy* remains a seminal civil rights and constitutional moment.

Yet for the students at the urban California middle school I just described, the struggle for education on equal terms seems to question the ruling in *Plessy* as much as it questions the promise of *Brown*. The students at UCMS, like millions of low-income students of color across the nation, are consigned to public schools that are *both* separate and unequal.

The struggle on behalf of students like those at UCMS is being waged today in state courts across the country. These are cases seeking adequate and equitable resources for all students. In what follows, I use *Williams v. California* as an example of this current struggle.[3] Mounted in the spirit of *Brown*, cases such as *Williams* continue the fight for education on equal terms. However, these cases also echo *Plessy*—they seek to make good on the stipulation that separate facilities must, at least, be equal. That *both* of these historic cases echo in today's courts speaks volumes about the past fifty years. In *Williams*, as in past cases, the claims of *Brown* and the stipulation of *Plessy* are both resisted strenuously. Research today, as in the past, plays a key role in school equity cases. However, in *Williams*, we are reminded that research can be used to eviscerate the very education for which people struggle.

Williams v. State of California was filed in the California Superior Court on May 17, 2000, the forty-sixth anniversary of the *Brown* decision. The case carries the name of Eliezer Williams, an African American student who attended a school like the one I described a minute ago. Nearly all of the forty-eight named student plaintiffs are Black, Latino, or Asian Pacific Islander, and they attend schools with predominantly non-White student bodies. Very large numbers of their classmates qualify for free or reduced-price meals, and a high percentage are still learning English.

The defendants are the governor of the State of California, the State Board of Education, and the superintendent of public instruction. They are represented by a high-priced private law firm, O'Melveny and Myers. The plaintiffs are represented through the pro bono work of Morrison and Foerster, and by a group of civil rights legal advocates including the American Civil Liberties Union; Public Advocates, Inc; Mexican American Legal and Education Fund; and other civil rights groups.

THE PLAINTIFFS' CLAIMS

The *Williams* plaintiffs claim that they and many other California children like them attend "schools that shock the conscience."[4] These are schools with conditions so poor that no academic, or lawyer, or politician would allow his or her own child to step foot inside them. In the words of the complaint, their schools lack "trained teachers, necessary educational supplies, classrooms, even seats in classrooms, and facilities that meet basic health and safety standards."[5]

The plaintiffs argue that, by permitting such schools, California's educational system fails to fulfill its constitutional obligation. In California, education is a fundamental right. California law also requires basic educational equality—that is, the state must provide all students with the essential elements of schooling that it provides to most students. Consequently, the *Williams* plaintiffs claim that there is a constitutional floor below which no California child's education should fall, and that their schools do not meet this test. They also claim that substandard schools are attended disproportionately by low-income African Americans and Latinos. The plaintiffs' complaint in *Williams* is fundamentally a *Plessy* complaint: Our schools are both separate and terribly unequal.

Notably, the Williams case is not a school funding case. What the plaintiffs seek is qualified teachers, a sufficient supply of instructional materials, and safe and healthy school buildings. They want a state educational system that ensures that all California students have these fundamental tools.

PLAINTIFFS' EXPERTS

The plaintiffs' attorneys asked a number of researchers to examine California's education system in light of the claims in the case. Over the course of a year or so, Linda Darling-Hammond, Michelle Fine, Norton Grubb, Kenji Hakuta, Rick Mintrop, Gary Orfield, Mike Russell, and I, among others, used existing research and data about California's schools to address four key questions:

- Are qualified teachers, appropriate instructional materials, and adequate school facilities essential?

- Is California currently providing them equally?
- Are California's policies adequate to prevent such problems, or discover and correct them if they should arise?
- Could the state do better?

To address the first question, the plaintiffs' experts began with California's content standards, the accountability tests linked to these standards, and the soon-to-be-implemented requirement making the high school diploma contingent upon students passing a standards-based exit exam.

The experts concluded that the essential educational resources and conditions are those necessary to give students a reasonable opportunity to learn the content and skills identified in the state's standards. These opportunities include, at the very least, qualified teachers (as defined by the state's teaching credentials), sufficient standards-aligned instructional materials, and safe, uncrowded facilities. Notably, the experts did not assert that the presence of teachers, books, and decent school buildings would *guarantee* high-quality schools or high student achievement. Rather, they contended that, without these basic tools, students face unreasonable barriers to their rightful education.

Answering the second question, the plaintiffs' experts found that teachers, books, and facilities both are in short supply and are less available to low-income students of color. They also found that these deficiencies are clustered and that their deleterious effects are compounded.

They concluded the problems to be so widespread that they point to systemic, state-level problems that local schools and districts could not reasonably be expected to surmount.

Let me give you just a flavor of the evidence.

Inequalities in Qualified Teachers. In 2001–2002, approximately 45,000 teachers were working in California Schools without full certification, a number that affects at least a million students. Some of these teachers were interns enrolled in a teacher preparation programs; some were pre-interns, still struggling to pass the subject-matter exams required to become an intern. Others were on emergency credentials or waivers. The underprepared teachers were concentrated in schools attended by minority students. Data shows that the schools with fewer qualified teachers are disproportionately located in neighborhoods where most residents are Latino and African American. In schools with more than 90 percent minority students, an average of 25 percent of the teachers lacked full certification.

Inequalities in Instructional Materials. The plaintiffs' experts also found that California schools suffer from significant shortages of instructional materials. In a 2002 survey of over a thousand California teachers, a third reported that they did not have enough textbooks for students to take home to do homework. The distribution of instructional materials is also unequal. Teachers in schools with the most Latino and African American students were nearly two times more likely to report that they have too few textbooks for students to take them home.

Inequalities in School Facilities. California's Proposition 13, passed in 1978, began an erosion of the educational infrastructure that has continued and worsened. Nowhere is that more obvious that in California's overcrowded and deteriorated school buildings. Plaintiffs' experts found that one in three students attend an overcrowded school or one that needs significant modernization. Some schools are in worse shape than others. In the 2002 survey, teachers in low socioeconomic status, high-minority schools rated their facilities as "poor" four times as often as teachers in schools with few minority students.

The state's inadequate facilities have also meant severe overcrowding. The state's most overcrowded schools enroll 150 percent of their capacity. They follow what the state calls a "Concept 6" calendar. This schedule cuts seventeen days from the school year in order to squeeze in three revolving tracks of students. These schools, when you look carefully at the data, again are concentrated in the neighborhoods with the highest concentration of Latino and African American families.

Inequalities Converge. Notably, the plaintiffs' experts also found that the inequalities in students' access to teachers, materials, and facilities converge. As at UCMS, schools with problems in one area tend to have problems in the others. Where you find poor facilities, you find shortages in high-quality materials. These are the very schools that have the most difficulty attracting and retaining qualified teachers.

Flaws in California's Education Policies. The plaintiffs' experts also found in the state's educational policies serious flaws that contribute to all these problems. The state has no policies that ensure that all students have qualified teachers, adequate textbooks, or decent school buildings. For example, California has fairly rigorous state policies governing teacher certification (policies that make clear the state's conviction that well-prepared teachers are an important element of educational opportunity). But nowhere does the state require that students actually be taught by a fully qualified teacher. In fact, California's Commission on Teacher Credentialing makes it quite easy for local districts to hire teachers without full certification. Similar problems plague the state's policies regarding textbooks and school facilities.

Making matters worse, there are no mechanisms to detect these problems or to intervene. The 2002 survey of teachers that provided these data was a private survey, made necessary by the fact that the state does not collect this information.

After reviewing policies in other states, the plaintiffs' experts recommended that California reconstruct its state policies in ways that would to prevent the problems that now plague its schools, and to discover and correct them, should they arise. They recommended that the state

- Set standards specifying that all students must have qualified teachers, sufficient instructional materials, and safe, uncrowded school buildings
- Base state funding on what these schooling essentials actually cost, and adjust those costs for the challenges in different communities
- Establish clear lines of state, regional, and district responsibility—where the buck stops, in other words
- Accountability for these basic resources, i.e., for students' "opportunities to learn"
- Intervene when schools fail to provide them.

With such policies, the plaintiffs' experts argued, the state could either prevent problems from occurring or correct them when they arise.

THE STATE'S DEFENSE

The state responded with a vigorous defense. It gathered its own set of experts to assess California's schools and to critique the plaintiffs' experts' studies. The state's experts include Russell Gersten, Eric Hanushek, Caroline Hoxby, Michael Podgursky, Margaret Raymond, Christine Rossell, Anita Summers, Herbert Walberg, and others.

These experts have reframed the case. They *do not* argue that all California's students have qualified teachers, instructional materials, and decent school buildings. What they *do* argue is that the state should be (and is) focused on increasing the "productivity" of its schools—their success in increasing achievement—and that qualified teachers, instructional materials, and decent school buildings aren't all that essential.

They also argue that increased productivity results from local school management and parent involvement. Action by the state to make schools equal in their basic resources would not only be ineffective, it might actually make schools worse. They argue that the best approach for the state to take is to continue its current standards and test-based accountability approach.

Finally, they declare not only that the plaintiffs' case is without merit but also that by bringing the case, the plaintiffs seek, illegitimately, to violate democratic processes.

Let's look more closely at this line of argument.

The resources of concern to the plaintiffs haven't been proven to increase school productivity. The first line of argument by the state's experts is that a particular school resource—i.e., qualified teachers, instructional materials, or buildings—is only essential, if there is evidence that the resource has an independent and positive effect on students' achievement. Further, evidence of this independent effect is only credible if produced by research using a narrow range of methods, preferably experiments or econometric statistical analyses.

They then assert that the plaintiffs' concerns are misplaced because neither the plaintiffs' experts, nor anyone else for that matter, have been able to show, using the proper methods, that qualified teachers, proper textbooks, or decent school buildings actually *cause* test scores to rise. As support, they draw on a tradition of production-function research, following Coleman's 1966 study that, they claim, finds no evidence that increases in educational resources cause increases in students' measured achievement.

It is to this tradition that state expert Erik Hanushek refers when he claims,

> many of the central theories and arguments advanced [by the plaintiffs] are directly contradicted by extensive research into the determinants of students' achievement.[6]

Not surprisingly, the state's experts do not discuss the many scholarly critiques of education production research. Moreover, in their own analyses, they depart from this standard they impose on the plaintiffs' experts.

To undermine the importance of teachers, for example, Margaret Raymond of the Hoover Institution argues,

> It simply cannot be the case that experienced teachers are important if it is possible to identify cases where they've not influenced the outcome of students.[7]

Expert Eric Hanushek argues that textbooks matter only in developing countries.

> Studies of the effects of textbooks find an impact only in places where the level of distribution of textbooks is radically different than found in California.[8]

Expert Christine Rossell claims that variations among California's schools don't influence student achievement.

> I have never seen a public school in California whose facilities were so bad that children could not learn in them.[9]

Expert Susan Phillips suggests that, if problems exist, they can be easily overcome:

> Though inconvenient, students can share books, use copied materials or Internet resources, wear coats in cold classrooms, or use a restroom on another floor.[10]

An Impossible Burden of Proof. Expert Raymond subjects the importance of teachers, instructional materials, and facilities to an impossible burden of proof. She argues that if one can find a single case where student learning occurred in the absence of resources specified in the plaintiffs' claim, it proves their lack of centrality to education:

> If the three inputs at issue in this case were essential, then it would not be the case that students and schools could overcome the odds of not having them.[11]

Additionally, Raymond argues that resources must have a uniform effect, and one that is more significant than other features of schooling:

> Even if the input standards proposed by plaintiffs do impact student achievement, the burden would still rest with them to prove that these factors were the most significant drivers of student outcomes and . . . that the magnitude of the effect was larger than other potential factors . . . [and] . . . that these elements are essential to all schools and to all students in the same way.[12]

Productivity Is a Function of Local Decisions and Conditions. Eric Hanushek, Caroline Hoxby, and Margaret Raymond all argue that productivity is a function of good local school management and parent involvement. They claim that, if the state held all schools to standards regarding teachers, instructional materials, and facilities, it would undermine local control. That would frustrate good managers and discourage parent involvement, which, in turn, would depresses achievement and provide destructive excuses for students' test scores. Hoxby asserts, for example,

> a good manager may find himself unable to use resources effectively because his local circumstances would dictate a different set of inputs and policies than those forced upon him. He or she may end up spending considerable time and energy finding ways to work around state-determined input policies and reallocate his or her resources toward more productive uses.[13]

In Raymond's opinion, requiring all schools to provide qualified teachers, proper materials, and adequate buildings would also jeopardize parent involvement:

> Further, plaintiffs' proposals disenfranchise parents. By claiming to know what is best for students, plaintiffs are removing the option for parents to be co-creators of the education programs that best meet the needs of their children. Dictating rigid practices and requirements signals to parents that their role is at best secondary and that the education of their children is best left to experts.[14]

In sum, the state's experts call the plaintiffs' recommendations a return to "failed input policies of the past" that would undermine student achievement.

The State's Proper Role Is to Create Incentives that Boost Local Productivity. Using theories of marketplace economics and a reward-and-punishment view of motivation, several of the experts argue strongly that good performance incentives, without new resources, can release the local creativity and effort that will make schools productive. Without such incentives, additional money spent on education will be wasted.

They go on to argue that California's current test-based accountability system has all the right incentives, and that it provides locals the flexibility they require. In fact, expert Herb Walberg judged California's policy system to be "near state of the art."

They do recognize, however, that California schools are not now performing as they should. But they claim that the state's accountability system has not been in place long enough to have its full salutary effect. They also assert that local factors over which the state has no control inhibit schools' performance. They blame

- Local mismanagement and weak motivation on the part of educators.
- Students' backgrounds—i.e., their poverty status, family values and practices, community and neighborhood resources, etc.

State expert Caroline Hoxby argues, for example,

In fact, the vast majority of variation in students' achievement is explained not by their schools, but by what their parents do and how much their neighborhood supports education.[15]

Hoxby supports her statement with her new analysis of NELS, from which she concludes that an astonishing 94 percent of students' achievement gains at the twelfth grade is a function of their family background. She credits the peer group for another 3 percent, leaving only 3 percent for anything they've experienced at school.

Objecting to Current Policies Subverts Democratic Processes. Finally, the State's experts assert that the plaintiffs, by bringing the case, seek to violate "democratic" processes of education policymaking. They argue that legislation, administrative regulation setting, local school boards, etc., are the means by which the people of California should (and do) establish the educational policies they prefer. Caroline Hoxby calls the plaintiffs "audacious" because they seek to "substitute their judgment for the judgment of Californians."[16] Raymond argues that

> their focus on forcing upward accountability through the California Department of Education is in complete disregard for the constitutional process in California for managing policy disputes, namely the election of the legislature and the governor.[17]

Finally, Rossell speculates that the plaintiffs have pursued the cases because they

> do not know how to achieve the lofty goals they propose within the constraints of an open, democratic political process where many competing individuals and groups have access to government.[18]

ECHOES OF *BROWN, PLESSY,* AND JIM CROW

Just below the surface of the arguments in *Williams* lie themes that run through the historic battle over the meaning of equality and the role of the state.

Parallels in the Plaintiffs' Cases. The plaintiffs in *Williams* follow the tradition begun by the NAACP in the many cases they mounted on their way to the *Brown* decision. In 1935, NAACP attorney Charles Houston presented evidence in *Murray v. Pearson* that the only college in which plaintiff Donald Murray could enroll—the Princess Anne Academy for Negroes—had a far less qualified faculty and inferior resources than the all-White University of Maryland Law School.[19] These inequalities violated the equal protection provision of the Fourteenth Amendment, Houston argued. Similarly, in 1946, Thurgood Marshall offered evidence in *Sweatt v. Painter* that the makeshift law school that Texas had established for Herman Sweatt—with three part-time instructors and three small basement rooms—violated Sweatt's right to an education equal to that provided by the all-white University of Texas Law School.[20]

Three of the school cases that were consolidated into *Brown* relied on testimony about deep inequalities in school resources and conditions. In *Briggs v. Elliott,* the South Carolina case, Professor Matthew Whitehead testified that his survey of Clarendon County schools showed that the Black schools

- were cheaply built, and lacked running water, indoor plumbing, and lunchrooms;
- had overcrowded classrooms with rough unfinished furniture,
- lacked essential instructional materials such as blackboards, charts, maps, globes, stereopticons, and more.[21]

In Wilmington, Delaware, the Black plaintiffs in *Belton v. Gebhart,* offered similar evidence. At the White schools

- school facilities were better built and had more space,
- teachers were far better educated, and
- the curriculum was much stronger than what was available at the Black schools.[22]

In *Davis v. the School Board of Prince Edward County,* Virginia, the NAACP offered evidence that the Black schools, unlike the White schools, had

- holes in the floor and heating problems,

- teachers who were paid less,
- a weak curriculum,
- a scarcity of books and equipment.[23]

Additionally, the Black high school had no gymnasium, cafeteria, auditorium with seats, or lockers. The temporary buildings constructed to accommodate the growing number of students were known as "tar paper shacks."

Although the ultimate goal in all of these cases was eliminating segregation, their arguments rested on evidence demonstrating that *Plessy*'s requirement of separate-but-equal was not being met—that schools for Black and White children were unequal in their most basic features.

As in the case of *Williams* today, key to these earlier cases was statistical evidence presented by social scientists proving broad patterns of inequality in racially segregated schools.

Parallels in the Defense—Unequal Resources. The state's defense in *Williams* takes a very different route than the defense against the pre-*Brown* cases, but it also echoes themes from those earlier arguments. The deflection of responsibility for inequalities from higher officials to local conditions has a decidedly familiar ring.

In South Carolina's *Briggs* case, for example, the defense claimed that the students' high truancy rate justified the large class sizes, and that the absence of running water and electricity at "colored" schools was understandable, given the lack of utilities in the countryside where Black children lived. In the Delaware *Belton* case, the defense argued that the inequalities were a function of the different communities in which students attended school. The superiority of White students' schools, the defense contended, "flow from living in the suburbs." The Blacks' misfortunes came from going to school in the city. In *Prince Edward County,* the defense argued that academic courses weren't offered in the Black high school because there was no demand for them. The presiding judge actually suggested that the differences in teachers' training and salaries weren't all that important to the quality of teaching.

However, *unlike* the experts in *Williams,* the defendants in these earlier cases acknowledged the importance of conditions and resources. Most defended themselves by pointing to progress. They touted new schools that were being built for Black students. They pointed to legislation equalizing salaries for Black and White teachers. They did not claim that the teachers, books, and school buildings really don't cause student achievement.

Parallels in the Defense—Local Control. The state's "local control" claim in *Williams* echoes the reasoning used by Supreme Court following the Civil War. Consistently, the post–Civil War courts argued that federal government intrusion to enforce Blacks' rights as citizens would have the effect of degrading state government. In the *Slaughter-house Cases* of 1872 and the *Civil Rights Cases* of 1883, for example, the Court ruled that the federal government had no authority to curb most civil rights violations. It was the states, not the federal government that had the authority and responsibility to grant or withhold citizen's rights. And, notably, in its 1896 ruling in *Plessy,* the Court delegated judgments about what constitutes separate-but-equal to local governments.

In the post-*Brown* era, Strom Thurmond, George Wallace, and others who favored segregation consistently used claims of "states' rights" to oppose the federal government's efforts to achieve greater racial equality.

Parallels in the Defense—Overriding the Will of the People. Finally, the claim by the *Williams* defense that the plaintiffs are using the courts to defy democracy—to circumvent the will of the majority—also hearkens to a century-old tradition of excusing civil rights violations in the name of public preferences.

In *Plessy,* for example, once the Court dismissed the claim that racially separate facilities violate the Constitution, it used a majoritarian standard to determine whether or not the segregation policy they were judging was reasonable:

> In determining the question of reasonableness, [the Court] is at liberty to act with reference to the established usages, customs, and traditions of the people, and with a view to the promotion of their comfort, and the preservation of the public peace and good order.[24]

The same thinking constrained the Court's ruling in *Mendez v. Westminster*—the 1947 case outlawing segregation in California. The Court ordered the desegregation of the Westminster schools on very narrow grounds: Westminster had violated the Fourteenth Amendment, only because California didn't have a law that permitted segregated Mexican schools. The Court refrained from ruling on "separate but equal" itself because it was unwilling to counter prevailing public attitudes. Judge Stevens wrote in the opinion,

> We are not tempted by the siren who calls to us that the sometimes slow and tedious ways of democratic legislation is [sic] no longer respected in a progressive society.[25]

WHY IS HISTORY REPEATING ITSELF?

It's sobering to recognize that the *Williams* plaintiffs and experts have mounted arguments and evidence as if *Plessy v. Ferguson* was still the prevailing ruling about educational equality. Why might this be the case?

Certainly one explanation is the courts' steady, thirty-year retreat from school desegregation as the preferred means for providing education on equal terms. Once we accept that schools are (and will remain) segregated, the next reasonable battle is to ensure equality in resources and conditions: If schools must be separate, then at least they should be equal.

Moreover, in California, the situation has deteriorated so much that civil rights attorneys are cautious about relying on the principled arguments about segregation and equality that lie deep within the structure of *Brown*. Instead, they rely on the mountains of data on tangible inequalities. It should be no surprise, then, that the *Williams* plaintiffs' arguments resemble the cases leading up to *Brown* when Thurgood Marshall and other NAACP attorneys felt that the courts simply weren't ready for principled arguments.

But how might we explain the parallels in the *Williams* defense arguments and those who sought to uphold Jim Crow schools? Local control is a powerful theme that Americans draw upon, one that often masks less palatable values. California's embrace of local control is a way of deflecting state responsibility, just as the Southern states embraced local control as a way of fending off federal interference.

In neither of these instances, however, was local control the real issue. The connection between the defense against *Williams* and the defense against *Brown* is the convenient and somewhat cynical use of local control as a façade to hide a less acceptable agenda. In *Williams* the state may be mainly concerned about the cost of providing all students an adequate education. Equity inevitably means more spending, which means higher taxes. In the pre-*Brown* days in the South, the defense of segregated schools was grounded in deep racial fears. California certainly cannot argue publicly, "We think money is wasted on those people," any more than Southern states could openly argue, "We won't abide racial mixing."

Finally, it's difficult to explain why the *Williams* defense experts would revisit the argument that the plaintiffs' claims are illegitimate because they seek to override public preferences. Surely they know that a central role of the courts is to adjudicate claims that the majority has violated the fundamental constitutional rights of individuals or politically powerless minorities. Perhaps they simply hope the California court, like those in *Plessy* and *Mendez*, will find this a convenient excuse to avoid enforcing the plaintiffs' claim to equal treatment by the state.

BROWN'S UNANSWERED QUESTION

So where does all this leave us? *Williams v. California* provides sobering evidence that, although much has changed since *Brown*, much of the underlying reasoning and prejudicial logic that shapes law and legislation remains the same.

Fifty years after *Brown*, the plaintiffs' complaint in *Williams* is fundamentally a *Plessy* complaint: our separate schools are unequal. More than a century after *Plessy*, the *Williams* defense recapitulates arguments that bolstered segregated and inferior schools and Jim Crow laws more generally.

However, *Williams* does not simply recapitulate the pre-*Brown* arguments over equality and the reach of the courts. It also reflects the nation's response to *Brown*. That racial segregation is not the issue at hand speaks loudly to the legal reversals and profound social disappointments of the past fifty years. The struggle for education "on equal terms" in twenty-first-century California is decidedly less ambitious, and perhaps less naïve, than it was in the pre-*Brown* South.

The *Williams* case also reflects the nation's shift to the political right regarding the role of government in education. The state's experts not only retreat from the principle that the state must guarantee educational equality, they also reject the idea that the state should be responsible for setting and enforcing basic standards of educational adequacy.

We should not be surprised. In other settings, several of the state's experts question the viability of state-provided education per se, preferring privatized, market-based approaches to education. Experts Hoxby, Hanushek, and Walberg, for example, are among the nation's foremost advocates for deregulation, choice, and privatization.

Perhaps we should also not be surprised that the state would adopt such arguments in its own defense. Given the undisputed low attainments of Latino and African American students and the popular rhetoric around the "achievement gap," the focus on schooling outcomes, rather than on resources, is attractive to many. Yet could it be that the state of California is willing to ignore (or dismiss) the obvious—that teachers, instructional materials, and facilities matter to learning? That the governor and the state's education leaders are content to allow California's increasingly segregated schools to remain so terribly unequal in these most fundamental features of schooling? That they actually consider test-based incentives an effective and constitutional tool to counter gross disparities in the education that the state provides to children?

These possibilities are particularly troubling, given that California is a state where education has been ruled a fundamental right under the Constitution. California is a state where the law defines educational equality as providing to all children the educational tools that are provided to most.

Today, the *Williams* case is at a standstill. Throughout his campaign for governor, Arnold Schwarzenegger derided the condition of California public schools, expressing outrage at the failure to provide the most vulnerable children with qualified teachers, sufficient instructional materials, and decent school buildings. Once in office, he made clear that the *Williams* case was not one he wanted to fight.

For months now, the plaintiffs' lawyers and the governor's team have been closeted in negotiations. Yet it remains to be seen whether a settlement can be reached between the state's Republicans and the ACLU-led litigation team. *So far, however, the governor has not rejected the defense mounted by the state's experts and all it implies about the struggle for education on equal terms.*

Whatever happens in *Williams,* however, the case is a powerful reminder of W. E. B. Du Bois's caution, written in 1954, only days after the *Brown* decision: "Great as is this victory, many and long steps on Freedom Road lie ahead."

POSTSCRIPT

In 2004 the plaintiffs in *Williams v. State of California* entered a settlement with the state in order to end the litigation. Pursuant to the settlement, the state passed what is commonly termed "Williams Settlement Legislation." This legislation mandated regular building repairs, clean and safe facilities, and sufficient and appropriate textbooks and instructional materials for all of California's public school students. Additionally, the legislation requires regular site visits and inspections of schools, as well as a uniform complaint process for parents, students, teachers, and community residents. Although the path to educational equity is far from complete in California, these measures have made a significant difference for California public school students and provide a useful model for future legislative and judicial remedies for school inequity. California community-based organizations continue to hold the state accountable under the terms of the legislation and encourage community members to utilize the terms of the settlement to advocate for the children of the state.

NOTES

1. *Brown v. Board of Education,* 347 U.S. 483, 493 (1954).
2. *Plessy v. Ferguson,* 163 U.S. 537 (1896).
3. *Williams v. State of California,* No. 312236 (Cal. Super. Ct., S.F. County, filed May 17, 2000).
4. First Amended Complaint for Injunctive and Declaratory Relief, *Williams v. State of California,* No. 312236 (Cal. Super. Ct., S.F. County, filed May

17, 2000), [hereinafter First Amended Complaint] at p. 6. This and other court papers are available in full at http://www.decentschools.com/court_ papers.php.

5. First Amended Complaint, at 6.

6. Expert Report of Erik Hanushek, *Williams v. State*, No. 312236 (Cal. Super. Ct., S.F. County, filed May 17, 2000), at 1 [hereinafter Hanushek]. This and all other expert reports are available in full at http://www.decentschools.com/ experts.php.

7. Expert Report of Margaret Raymond, *Williams v. State*, No. 312236 (Cal. Super. Ct., S.F. County, filed May 17, 2000), at 8 [hereinafter Raymond].

8. Hanushek, at 12.

9. Expert Report of Christine Rossell, *Williams v. State*, No. 312236 (Cal. Super. Ct., S.F. County, filed May 17, 2000), at 22 [hereinafter Rossell].

10. Expert Report of Susan Phillips, *Williams v. State*, No. 312236 (Cal. Super. Ct., S.F. County, filed May 17, 2000), at 74-75 [hereinafter Phillips].

11. Raymond, at 11.

12. Ibid., at 8, 11.

13. Expert Report of Caroline Hoxby, *Williams v. State*, No. 312236 (Cal. Super. Ct., S.F. County, filed May 17, 2000), at 5 [hereinafter Hoxby].

14. Raymond, at 18.

15. Hoxby, at 11.

16. Hoxby, at 1.

17. Raymond, at 5.

18. Rossell, at 34.

19. *Murray v. Pearson* 169 Md. 478, 182 A. 590 (1936).

20. *Sweatt v. Painter* 339 U.S. 629 (1950).

21. See *Briggs v. Elliott*, 347 U.S. 483 (1954).

22. Richard Kluger. *Simple Justice: The History of* Brown v. Board of Educa- tion *and Black America's Struggle for Equality* (New York: Random House, 1975), 423–33 (discussing *Gebhart v. Belton*, 91 A.2d 137 (Del. Ch. 1952)).

23. Kluger, 458–79 (discussing *Davis v. School Board of Prince Edward County*, 103 F. Supp. 33 [D. Va. 1952]).

24. *Plessy v. Ferguson*, 163 U.S. 537 (1896).

25. Charles M. Wollenberg. *All Deliberate Speed: Segregation and Exclusion in California Schools, 1855–1975* (Berkeley: University of California Press, 1976), 129–30 (quoting *Mendez v. Westminster School District*, 161 F.2d 774, 779–81 [9th Cir. 1947]).

4

Constitutional Property v.
Constitutional People

Robert P. Moses

In his essay, Bob Moses identifies the African American struggle
to move from property to citizenship through the lenses of four
historic periods, the late-eighteenth century, the late-nineteenth
century, the mid-twentieth century civil rights movement era, and
the contemporary period. He demonstrates two dominant and
conflicting interpretations of the provisions of the Fourteenth
and Fifteenth Amendments, the amendments that confer equal
protection and suffrage rights upon African Americans, a conflict
that continues to this day. He argues that the just interpretation,
the one which supports the status of full citizenship for African
Americans, has only succeeded on the legislative front when it is
demanded by activism, collaboration, and service. And finally,
Moses identifies education as a principal terrain upon which the
denial of citizenship has occurred for African Americans, and
a necessary ground for continued struggle.

—Editors

AN EIGHTEENTH-CENTURY SLAVE PERSONAGE

In 1749, a West African boy, nine years old and captured, sailed the
middle passage to Virginia and survived. In August of that year, a
Scottish-born merchant slave trader, twenty-four years old and up
and coming, peered into the pluck of that nine-year-old and bought
him. Charles Stewart took the boy, Somerset, as his personal slave.[1]
Twenty years passed, and twenty-nine-year-old Somerset accompanied Stewart to London to help care for Stewart's sister's family when
her husband died. London, in 1769, was awash with Africans from
the British Empire: slaves and runaways, beggars and workers, sea-

men and artisans. Two years later Somerset, while running errands for his master—meeting Blacks on the streets, in the stores, along the docks—crafted a way out of slavery and bondage. He arranged to be baptized as James Somerset, acquired two English godparents, Thomas Walkin and Elizabeth Cade, and flowed into what I call the "IRS," London's stream of "Insurgent Runaway Slaves." Stewart, feeling "betrayed and publicly insulted," posted notices, and on November 26, 1771, slave catchers delivered Somerset to a ship bound for Jamaica.

Seven days later, Somerset's godmother petitioned the oldest and highest common law court in England for a writ of habeas corpus to release James Somerset. Lord Mansfield, the Chief Justice of King's Court, issued the writ and six days later, on December 9, 1771, James Somerset appeared before the bench where a Captain Knowles declared: "Charles Stewart, a colonial from America, deposited his slave, Somerset, aboard the *Ann and Mary,* to be sold in Jamaica."[2]

Lord Mansfield suggested Somerset be set free and released him pending a hearing. When West Indian planters pushed for a decision upholding slavery to stabilize prices in the commodities markets, Lord Mansfield cautioned them: "If they think the question of great commercial concern is . . . the only method of settling the point for the future . . . they should prepare an application to Parliament."[3]

But Parliament was content to let the matter rest in the court and refused the merchants a hearing. In late May, a month before the hearing took place, a London newspaper opined: "If the laws of England do not confirm the colony laws with respect to property in slaves, no man of common sense will, for the future, lay out his money in so precarious a commodity."[4]

On June 22, 1772, the clerk called the case of "James Somerset, a Negro on Habeas Corpus," and Lord Mansfield mounted the bench, bewigged, and delivered his judgment:

> The state of slavery is of such a nature, that it is incapable of being introduced on any reasons, moral or political . . . it's so odious, that nothing can be suffered to support it but positive law. Whatever inconveniences, therefore, may fol-

low from the decision, I cannot say this case is allowed or approved by the law of England; and therefore the black must be discharged.[5]

Black members in the audience rose and bowed; newly awakened nieces and nephews in England decided to pay Uncle Somerset a visit.

In Colonial America, a planter, Gabriel Jones, included the following alert in a notice posted to help capture an IRS named Bacchus: "It is probable he may endeavor to get on board some vessel bound for Great Britain, from a knowledge he has of the late determination of Somerset's case."[6] The IRS spirit was catching.

But we should consider the question: Why did Stewart feel "betrayed and publicly humiliated" by Somerset? In his opinion, Stewart had done everything imaginable for Somerset, but his imagination could not access Lord Mansfield's peripheral vision of the human playing field and acknowledge Somerset, his slave person, as a citizen person. Somerset must have been so relaxed in his persona as Stewart's personal slave and so in charge of his slightest mannerisms as to leave Stewart clueless about his coming apostasy. Stewart had been "taken" by Somerset.

The issue reached across the Atlantic into Colonial Revolutionary America, where colonialists who could not imagine their slaves as constitutional people required an explicit declaration of "positive law" to protect their constitutional property.

There is a "Somerset clause"[7] in the nation's Constitution: Article IV, Section 2, paragraph 3. At the 1787 Constitutional Convention, discriminating men, determined to establish a "workable government," peered through the cataracts on their imaginations and burned into the Constitution a stigma about their constitutional property:

> No person held to service or labor in one state, under the laws thereof, escaping into another,
> shall, in consequence of any law or regulation therein, be discharged from such service or labor,
> but shall be delivered up on claim of the party to whom such service or labor is due.

THE NINETEENTH CENTURY: THE WAR
OVER BLACK PEOPLE AS CONSTITUTIONAL
PROPERTY, AND ITS AFTERMATH

Such property-holding men established a government that "worked" for seventy-five years. They then declared war on one another in 1862 over that bit of "positive law" about constitutional property. After their war, they returned to the task of establishing a "workable government" around a dedicated Jim Crow line: On the one hand the Mason-Dixon line became a kind of continental gutter to flush racism into the nation's basin. On the other hand it became a kind of continental ribbon with which to wrap up the nation's politics. The war forced concepts of betrayal and public humiliation on either side of this border of the two flags, albeit attached to different emotions.

South of the Mason-Dixon line, "Redeemers,"[8] deprived of Africans as constitutional property, turned their humiliation into outrage, terrorism, and Jim Crow. They imagined freed Africans to be "niggers"—niggers, unlike property, being worthy of lynching. North of the Mason-Dixon line, "Reconcilers," decided, "We have done enough for them" and turned their feelings of betrayal and frustration into "workable government." Jim Crow and its dedicated line lasted another seventy-five years, until Negro college insurgents demolished it with sit-ins in the 1960s.

Jim Crow laws were a living institution. Unlike feudal laws, they did not assign the subordinate group a fixed status in society. Instead,

> They were constantly pushing the Negro farther down. . . . Its spirit is that of an all-absorbing autocracy of race, an animus of aggrandizement which makes, in the imagination of the white man, an absolute identification of the stronger race with the very being of the state.[9]

The project of Jim Crow also included education from the very beginning. In 1868, the South Carolina Constitution stated in Article XI; Sec. 7: "Separate schools shall be provided for children of the white and colored races, and no child of either race shall be permitted to attend a school provided for children of the other race."

In 1931 Arkansas declared the following in Statutory provision: Act #169; Acts of 1931; Sec. 97:

> The board of school directors of each district in the state shall be charged with the following powers and perform the following duties.
>
>   C. Establish separate schools for white and colored persons

Between 1868 and 1931 eighteen states—all of the South and as far north as Delaware and as far west as Arizona—made separation of the "colored and white races" in the public schools mandatory. Four states had laws *permitting* the separation of Whites and Blacks: Kansas, New Mexico, New York, and Wyoming.

Fifteen states did not address the matter at all, and for these the courts held that they could not separate Whites and Blacks. And ten states explicitly *forbad* the separation of Whites and Blacks (Negroes) in public schools: California, Illinois, Maine, Massachusetts, Nevada, New Jersey, Oregon, Pennsylvania, Rhode Island, and Washington.

School segregation laws and policies were mirrored by the denial of suffrage rights. The political conflict that laid the foundation for this denial, which stood through the better part of the twentieth century, occurred in 1875.

In February 1875, a Congressional committee reported on its investigations into the election in Vicksburg in 1874. The minority report filed by Democrats noted that

> A little learning is a dangerous thing in its application to Negroes. The educated among them are the most dangerous class in the community, as they exercise a malign and blighting influence over the future prospects of their race.[10]

The majority report, filed by Republicans, challenged the nation directly:

> One of two things this Nation must do: It must either restrain by force these violent demonstrations by the bold fierce spirits of the whites; it must, by the exercise of all its power, if needed, secure to every man, black and white, the free exercise

of the elective franchise, and punish, sternly and promptly, all who violently invade those rights; or it must say to the enfranchised voters of the South . . . we have made you men and citizens . . . we have given you the right to bear arms and to vote; now work out your own salvation as others have done; fight your way up to full manhood, and prove yourselves worthy of the endowments you have received at our hands. It is for the country to decide which is the best. But the country must decide quickly.[11]

In 1875, the national gutter that came to be the Jim Crow line was established in Mississippi when, emboldened by the events in Vicksburg the previous fall, Democrat "Redeemers" terrorized the freed slaves and ran them completely out of the political system. The following summer the Senate select committee came to Mississippi, took testimony all over the state, and issued the Boutwell Report. A quarter of a century later, in his memoirs, Senator George Boutwell of Massachusetts remarked, "For myself I had no doubt that the election of 1875 was carried by the Democrats by a preconceived plan of riots and assassinations."[12]

In 1907, Senator Benjamin Ryan "Pitchfork Ben" Tillman of South Carolina took the floor of the Senate to memorialize the execution of Mississippi's plan in South Carolina during the ill-fated presidential election of 1876, stating, "It was then that we shot them; it was then that we killed them; it was then that we stuffed ballot boxes; it was a fight between barbarism and civilization, between the African and the Caucasian for mastery."[13] "Pitchfork Ben" was telling the story of the nation, its fate, that which "confers and withdraws meaning or sense"[14] to its history on the floor of its Senate: There was a clear causal chain, from Grant's deciding in 1875 not to do what was needed to have a free election in Mississippi, to the Democrats' taking that state, to the Mississippi events emboldening Democrats in South Carolina, Florida, and Louisiana to try to win in the same way the Mississippi Democrats had.[15]

What followed was the national political compromise of 1877:

The Democrats agreed to let Rutherford Hayes (the Republican governor of Ohio) become president and the Republicans agreed in return to remove the remaining federal troops from the South. Reconstruction, which had wound up producing a lower-intensity continuation of the Civil War, was over. The South had won. And the events in Mississippi in 1875 had been the decisive battle.[16]

THE TWENTIETH CENTURY: THE FIGHT
FOR CONSTITUTIONAL CITIZENSHIP
IN HOUSING AND EDUCATION

In the fall of 1944, an estimated three thousand people gathered at the Hopson plantation outside of Clarksdale to watch eight bright red machines pick forty-two acres of cotton. Richard Hopson ran the plantation office and the previous spring he had penned a letter urging all the plantation owners in the Delta to "change as rapidly as possible from sharecropping to complete mechanized farming . . . to alleviate the Negro problem."

Three years later, David Cohn, who argued that the "taboos and conventions" of the Southern Whites would "keep the races separate from the cradle to the grave" put the following dilemma to the nation: "Five million people will be removed from the land within the next few years. They must go somewhere. But where? They must do something. But what? They must be housed. But where is the housing?"[17]

One answer was found in migration and public housing. In December of 1946, the Chicago Housing Authority moved a few Black families into a new housing project called Airport Homes, which was in a White neighborhood on the Southwest side. The Housing Authority proceeded with some care: it obtained the blessing of the mayor; it carefully screened the Black families; it moved them in during working hours, when the men in the neighborhood were away. Still, more than a thousand Whites gathered to "greet" the Black families. The mayor had to send in four hundred policemen to maintain order; the rioting went on and after two weeks the Black families moved out. Chicago maintained its housing color line.

Ten years later, after the 1954 Supreme Court's *Brown v. Board of Education* decision, "Willis wagons" maintained the school color line. It is obvious in retrospect that the established Black neighborhoods were far too small to hold all the Black people leaving Mississippi's plantations for Chicago but the Mayor's efforts were directed at finding ways to maintain the color line. Ben Willis, his school superintendent was immediately faced with the problem of severe overcrowding in the Black schools. Instead of integrating the adjacent and usually half-empty White schools, Willis put the Black schools on double shifts, eight to noon and noon to four, and installed "Willis Wagons" —trailers converted into temporary classrooms—in their playgrounds, thereby creating an urban equivalent of the inferior rural Black school systems of the South. Sharecropper education transferred into urban, northern America.

When the nation established sharecropping as an economic system tied to Jim Crow after its Civil War, it also established "sharecropper education," institutionalized in separate, inferior, and demeaning public schools for descendents of freed slaves in the plantation culture across the Black belt of the South where, as of 1930, 79 percent of their nearly twelve million descendents lived.[18]

Those five million people David Cohn preached about who were "removed from the land" between 1944 and 1970 were five million sharecroppers taking refuge in every major urban area, where, as Conant discerned, the nation's caste system, revealed itself most plainly in their schools.

James Bryant Conant introduced the SAT and ETS to the nation's universities during his two decades as president of Harvard (1933–1953). He published a book in 1961, *Slums and Suburbs,* in which he contrasted the picture of schools in the slums of big cities of the country with affluent suburban schools:

As I read the history of the U.S., this republic was born with a congenital defect—Negro slavery. Or, if one prefers another metaphor, we started life under a curse from which we are not yet free.

After the victory of the North . . . the people of the U.S. through their duly elected representatives in Congress acquiesced for generations in the establishment of a tight caste system as a substitute for Negro slavery. As we now recognize so plainly, but so belatedly, a caste system finds its clearest manifestation in an educational system.[19]

After World War II, the G.I. bill granted veterans access to a college education with no SAT tests to pass and no freshman evaluation standards. It was a true expansion of education into the White working class, accompanied by access to mortgages, the construction of the federal highway system and the building of the nation's suburbs for White people. Here was a Marshall Plan for White WWII veterans that left Jim Crow and the color line intact.

The educational caste system of the twentieth century north and south shows that just as Rome didn't collapse all at once, neither did slavery. The chaos of its aftermath mutated into that "all-absorbing autocracy of race" called Jim Crow and the fertile marriage of two flags flying high over a caste system maintained by sharecropper education. In the twentieth century, as in the nineteenth, the education caste system mirrored larger political struggles.

At the Delta town of Indianola, in the spring of 1955, in the aftermath of the 1954 Supreme Court school desegregation decision, *Brown v. Board of Education,* Mississippi launched its second plan: the White Citizens Councils and the doctrine of duplicitous terror as the appropriate response to the Court's decision exactly eighty years after Senator George Boutwell reported to the nation "that the election of 1875 was carried by the Democrats by a preconceived plan of riots and assassinations." From the 1955 gunning of Rev. George Lee in Belzoni, Mississippi, to the 1968 assassination of Martin Luther King, duplicitous terror caught up with "all deliberate speed" to confer onto and withdraw from the nation forty of freedom's insurgents, some well-known, others obscure.

Amzie Moore called the shootings "the modern politics": murder by gun as the modern form of lynching, dissecting for me a theory and practice of freedom, which, for him was the theory and practice of "race men," the way they carried the nation's fate: Amzie, C. C. Bryant, Webb Owens, E. W. Steptoe, Vernon Dahmer, Hartman Turnbow, Mr. Saunders of Greenwood, Aaron Henry and Medgar Evers, among others in Mississippi's "known world" who were race men. C. C., who died in McComb, Mississippi, in 2008, was perhaps the "last race man" because the concept and the phrase itself belong to the era of defiant Jim Crow, post Civil War and pre-sit-in movement. The great synergy of the Mississippi Movement flowed out of the marriage between the Student Nonviolent Coordinating Committee's sit-in energy and the "lived lives" of this handful of Mississippi NAACP race men. In the '60s we became daughters and sons in the house of their struggle.

MY STORY IN THE MOVEMENT

In the years following WWII, the overwhelming majority of Blacks were sharecroppers or just emerging from Jim Crow life, but not all, and in those years the nation began to search for its potential, Black as well as White. As I turned twelve, in January 1947, and graduated from the sixth grade in New York City, I was swooped into a special class to finish junior high school in two and one-half years instead of three, then passed, by exam, into Stuyvesant High School and, three years later, escorted, by grants, into the class of 1956 at Hamilton College, one of just two Blacks in a class of 125 males.

I got to Mississippi Delta civil rights activist Amzie Moore via Pop and Uncle Bill, Wyatt T and Bayard Rustin, Jane and Ella. Pop, my father, worked at the 369th Armory in Harlem, punching the watchman's stations, keeping the cavernous rooms presentable, shoveling snow off miles of sidewalk on cold winter days. I grew up hanging a lot with Pop, who liked to hang with people, and absorbed in this way earfuls of common-sense talk. Pop's best friend was his older brother Bill, and when the lightning stroke of the sit-ins startled the nation and woke me up too, I took off for Hampton Institute, where Uncle Bill headed the Department of Architecture, to check it out.

Students at Hampton were sitting-in at the Woolworth store in Newport News when I marched over with them and listened at the mass meeting where Wyatt T. Walker, down from Petersburg, announced the formation of a Harlem office for Martin.

Back home in New York, I jumped on the 7th Avenue train every afternoon after teaching math at the Horace Mann School in Riverdale, got off at 125th Street and Broadway and walked a few blocks to volunteer at the Northern support office for the Southern Christian Leadership Conference (SCLC), set up to support the work of Martin Luther King. Bayard Rustin ran the office, and I walked the streets of Harlem putting posters on lamp posts to announce the event at the 369th, where Pop worked, featuring Harry Belafonte and

Sidney Poitier, and where I was to see Malcolm X talking with Ossie Davis.

I asked Bayard to set me up with SCLC that summer and he sent me to Ella Baker. I saved up my money and took off for Atlanta. When I got there Ella was on a field trip, so I spent my first week stuffing envelopes for SCLC while talking about and meeting with insurgents from the Atlanta sit-in movement: Julian Bond and Ruby-Doris Smith. But it was Jane who explained to me about the Student Non-Violent Coordinating Committee (SNCC). Jane Stembridge, a young White student at Union Theological Seminary in New York, went to the meeting at Shaw University that Ella organized for the leadership of the sit-in insurgency:

> 1960 was the year of the massive awakening for the Negroes of the South—indeed Negro Americans generally. On February 1 of that year, four Negro college boys, freshmen at the Agricultural and Technical College in Greensboro, North Carolina, asked politely for coffee at Woolworth's lunch counter and continued to sit in silent protest when refused. The "sit-in," nemesis of Jim Crow, was born.[20]

At the meeting on Shaw's campus, Ella helped fashion a space for untapped sit-in insurgents to think for themselves, to make their own plans, to execute their own strategies:

> In April the SNCC ["Snick"] was formed—small, militant, very youthful, largely Negro, and Negro-led . . . Negroes were in charge of their own movement now and youth was in the vanguard.[21]

That summer, Jane and Ella sent me on a scouting trip through Alabama, Mississippi, and Louisiana. I met Fred Shuttlesworth in Birmingham, Aaron Henry in Clarksdale, Medgar Evers in Jackson, and Dr. Gilbert Mason in Biloxi, but it was Amzie Moore in the Mississippi Delta who was waiting with a plan to channel the energy of the Snick insurgents and turn Mississippi around.

After Jane and Ella sent me that summer to meet Amzie, I had one year to go to complete a three-year contract teaching middle school math at the Horace Mann School in New York. I saved my money and returned to the Delta a "Freedom Rider." John Lewis, Diane Nash and the Nashville student sit-in movement had carried the sit-in energy into Mississippi on a Greyhound bus and every Black-hued kid on a dusty Mississippi street could spot a "Freedom Rider" a block away. "Freedom fighters" burned a Greyhound bus carrying sit-in insurgents in Anniston, Alabama, in the spring of 1961 and with a measured response, the sit-in insurgency created "Freedom Riders," interstate travelers into terror who landed, of all places, in the Delta at Parchman, Mississippi's State Penitentiary, just a few miles from Cleveland, Amzie's home town.

We were Freedom's Riders in a nation "reconciled" to a culture of freedom that flew two flags over two "adjudicated" Constitutions: did the Fourteenth Amendment establish "ex-slaves and all Blacks to be full citizens by reaffirming universal guarantees implicit in the original Constitution and by making the federal government responsible for ensuring compliance by the states with those universal guarantees"?[22] Or, was the Fourteenth Amendment never properly ratified: "One flag's illegal powerplay on another flag's constitutional property"?[23]

Did the Fifteenth Amendment establish for Blacks the same rights to the vote as had been established for Whites? Or was the nation's system of federalism protected since 1875 "by non-recognition of federally guaranteed rights"[24]?

On an evening in September 1961 I was standing with John Hardy and Jess Brown, his lawyer, in the Federal District courtroom of Judge Cox. Hardy had accompanied farmers from Walthall County to the registrar's office in Tylertown on September 7, and when the registrar, John Q. Wood, refused permission to register, Hardy asked him, "Why?" Wood then reached into his drawer, ordered Hardy out at gunpoint and whipped the back of his head with a pistol as he was leaving. Out in the street, Hardy was arrested by the sheriff and charged with resisting arrest, inciting a riot, and disorderly conduct. We were in Judge Cox's court the evening before the trial, which was to begin the next morning in Tylertown at 9:00 a.m. Burke Marshall had sent John Doar to Judge Cox to seek a dismissal of all the charges. We waited as Judge Cox unceremoniously refused his request.

Hardy and I took off for Tylertown while Doar, in consultation with Burke, telephoned Justice Reeves of the fifth circuit court of appeals, who agreed to review the proceedings late that night. Doar hired a private plane, invited Mississippi's Attorney General to travel with him, and took off to Montgomery, Alabama, for an extraordinary midnight session about the reach of the Constitution and the nation's two flags for Freedom. Hardy and I spent the night at C.C. Bryant's home in McComb, got up early, drove to Tylertown and climbed the stairs to sit, out of sight, in the "buzzard's nest" for Negroes, a shelf up in the back of the empty courtroom. At 9:00 a.m., a lawyer came in to announce to a courtroom, now packed with White men, that the Department of Justice had obtained a temporary injunction to halt the proceedings against Hardy. We hit the stairs to the street, hustled to our car, and took off as a wave of White men from the courthouse descended. Burke eventually argued and won the case before a three-judge panel of the fifth circuit.[25] The presumption of innocence is not just a legal concept—and what a difference a "bureaucrat" makes.

For me, no one in Mississippi understood Jim Crow better than Amzie. Amzie's world became my world, and in the early darkness of a winter evening in February 1963, Jimmy Travis slipped behind the wheel and Randolph Blackwell crowded me beside him in a Snick Chevy in front of the Voter Registration Office in Greenwood, Mississippi, to take off for Greenville on U.S. Highway 82, straight across the Delta. Jimmy zigzagged out of town to escape an unmarked car, but as we headed west on 82, it trailed us and swept past near the turn off for Valley State University, firing automatic weapons and pitting the Chevy with bullets. Jimmy cried out and slumped; I reached over to grab the wheel and fumbled for the brakes as we glided off 82 into the ditch, our windows blown out, a bullet caught in Jimmy's neck.

After Jimmy caught that bullet in his neck, Snick regrouped to converge on Greenwood, and Black sharecroppers lined up at the courthouse to demand their right to vote. When Snick field secretaries were arrested, Burke Marshall, the Assistant Attorney General for Civil Rights under Robert F. Kennedy, removed our cases to the Federal District Court in Greenville and sent John Doar to be our lawyer. From the witness stand I looked out at a courtroom packed with Black sharecroppers from Greenwood, hushed along its walls, packed on its benches, and attended to the question put by Federal District Judge Clayton: "Why are you taking illiterates down to register to vote?" To whom had he put his question? The sharecroppers? Perhaps. We told him, in effect, that the country couldn't have its cake and eat it too.

We reminded him "playing fair" was also "playing American." The nation couldn't deny a whole people access to education and literacy and then turn around and deny them access to politics because they were illiterate.

But perhaps the inquiry was his own silent observation dressed up in a rhetorical question: *constitutional strangers are pressing against the Constitutional gate; however, the gate won't give, not on my watch.*

Destabilizing Jim Crow required earned insurgencies. The sit-in insurgents had to earn a platform to put their issues on the nation's table. They had to summon their human dignity to face down the South's psychological contempt and physical brutality and to call up the nation's common humanity. In Mississippi, we had to bide our time and learn to walk like trees between endless conversations that ended, "Well, I 'reckn' . . . ," to transfer the energy of the sit-ins into the "known world" of sharecropping, to reach across many frontiers to the sharecroppers in that Federal District Courtroom. First and foremost, we had to earn their respect and trust to get them to risk their livelihoods if not their lives. The idea was simple: get back up every time you get knocked down.

We also had to earn the respect of the Justice Department civil rights lawyers. Thanks to President Eisenhower and the 1957 Civil Rights Act, when Mississippi locked us up for working on voter registration, the Feds could set us free. But nothing required Burke and the Justice Department to turn that jailhouse key.

Even so, as the federal district judge reminded the Delta sharecroppers, if we were no longer constitutional property, we were not yet constitutional people. In his book, Burke Marshall credits a fallen president as having imagined just this outcome for the nation:

> The President [Kennedy] went further to seek a national commitment to meet the moral dilemma caused by the effects of our historical acceptance of a caste system weighted against Negroes. . . . In a series of White House meetings, he asked the help of all segments of national leadership, public and private, in facing such deep economic, social and educational racial problems as those of the great cities where federal, state and municipal policy in general coalesce, rather than clash, but no solution is yet in sight.[26]

In 1963, Byron De La Beckwith's murder of Medgar Evers jolted Allard Lowenstein and Robert Spike into Mississippi. They were both shocked into action. Al eventually led the first delegations of White college students into the state for the freedom vote in which COFO (Council of Federated Organizations) sponsored Aaron Henry and Ed King as governor and lieutenant governor in a freedom campaign, thereby introducing the concept that led to Freedom Summer in 1964. Robert brought the resources of the National Council of Churches into the orbit of the Mississippi movement to support Freedom Summer and direct crucial lobbying efforts in Midwest Republican congressional districts to help pass the Civil Rights Bill of 1964.

Beckwith may have planned Medgar's murder, but he, and all the rejoicing Redeemers, did not, could not, imagine how quickly events would move because of it. Neither could we, who gathered on Farish Street for Medgar's funeral and watched John Doar, his back to an arsenal of Mississippi's law enforcement troops, convince Ida Mae Holland from Greenwood, and all those with her, not to walk into "sure gunfire," into "things fall apart," into "national disaster." We were *all* navigating our rafts in the rapids of history's currents and couldn't quite imagine how things and people would "come together" from all over the South, as well as such Northern locales as Washington, D.C., and Chicago.

Thirty-plus Black high school graduates and college students came together in that pressured space-time to work "twenty-four seven," to get knocked down and get back up, to steady watch the Feds turn that jailhouse key; invisible to the nation at large to this day, ours was the sit-in energy translated into Amzie's world. We carved out the larger space in which Mickey and Rita Schwerner could operate in Meridian. It was we who called forth that remarkable network of Black Mississippi-matured women: Victoria Adams from Hattiesburg, Fannie Lou Hamer from Ruleville, Annie Devine from Canton, Hazel Palmer from Jackson, and Unita Blackwell from the Delta, who carried the Mississippi Freedom Democratic Party (MFDP) into the 1964 Democratic Convention in Atlantic City and broke the back of eighty-nine years of White-only Mississippi Democrats' party power. Snick was the heart and soul of the insurgency against Jim Crow, and these few dozen, the heart and soul of the Mississippi insurgency, came together and earned the right to call on the whole country's common humanity to bring down Jim Crow Mississippi.

It was only the penetration of the sit-in energy—first through the Freedom Rides and, under Amzie's guidance, the insurgency for the right to vote, and then, led by Snick, through the challenge of the Mississippi Freedom Democratic Party to the credentials committee at the 1964 National Democratic Convention—that broke the back of Mississippi's politics of duplicitous terror, where the State Sovereignty Commission made monthly payments to the White Citizens Councils who silenced the "good" folks and terrorized the "bad." This cleared the way for the voting rights legislation of 1965 to enable White and Black history-making Mississippi voters to jointly represent their state at the 1968 National Democratic Convention in Chicago. As the *New York Times* editorialized on August 27, 1964:

> The Freedom Democrats proved that a moral argument, if powerful enough and presented with dramatic force, can cut through the cynicism and frivolity that usually prevail in a convention atmosphere. . . . The day of the lily-white delegations from the South is over. The Democrats from the rest of the country have finally lost patience with the exclusion of Negroes from party affairs in the South.[27]

The Jim Crow ribbon around the nation's party structure was untied, but as we shall see, like Rome and slavery, Jim Crow did not collapse all at once. Amzie said it one thousand times if he said it once, "We are fighting to be first-, not second-class, citizens." The freedom of White people to own Blacks as constitutional property was abolished by the Civil War, but both flags still fly, and I find in the nation's constitution a context to relate to Amzie's concept of first-class citizenship: the idea that we are in struggle to evolve ourselves as constitutional people.

The Voting Rights Act of 1965 did not include literacy restrictions, and John Doar has a picture in his office of himself accompanying Attorney General Nicholas Katzenbach and Thurgood Marshall to defend the literacy provisions of the Voting Rights Act before the Supreme Court. Congress determined in 1965 that such a far-reaching statute was required as a response to compelling evidence of continuing interference with attempts by African American citizens to exercise their right to vote.

The Supreme Court, responding to opinions obtained from the Fifth Circuit Court of Appeals stated

> The enforcement clause of the Fifteenth Amendment gives Congress full remedial powers to prevent racial discrimination in voting. The Voting Rights Act is a legitimate response to the insidious and pervasive evil which has denied Blacks the right to vote since the adoption of the Fifteenth Amendment in 1870.[28]

All of this set the stage for the twenty-first century and our current national divide over education and the Fourteenth Amendment.

THE TWENTY-FIRST CENTURY

The nation flies two flags of freedom over two adjudicated constitutions. Was the Civil Rights Act of 1964 a piece of affirmative action legislation to protect, ninety-six years after its introduction, the instantaneous national citizenship acquired by a whole race of people in virtue of an "affirmative grant by the nation"? Or is it positive law all the way down?

> As for the Fourteenth Amendment, the tragic truth is that the amendment was never legally ratified . . . in the 96 years that have since elapsed, the Supreme Court has refused to accept for hearing any case protesting the illegality of the "ratification of the 14th Amendment."[29]

Is there common law to establish a conceptual framework for the common humanity of the "People of the United States"? Or is it each flag for itself and positive law as long as the nation shall endure? Did the Fourteenth Amendment establish national citizenship for Blacks to be protected by "Congressional legislation of a primary and direct character?" Or has the "first clause of the first section" been rightfully protected since 1883 by non-recognition?

On Friday, June 29, 2007, the *New York Times* spread pictures of all nine Supreme Court Justices on the front page to alert the nation of the "Bitter Division" at the Court over "*Brown* and the 14th Amendment." In the words of Harvard law professor Laurence H. Tribe, "There is a historic clash between two dramatically different visions not only of *Brown,* but also the meaning of the Constitution."[30]

Trent Lott embarrassed the Republican Party and annoyed much of the nation in December 2002, at the one hundredth birthday celebration for the retiring senator Strom Thurmond, with this tribute:

> I want to say this about my state: when Strom Thurmond ran for president [1948] we voted for him. We're proud of it. And if the rest of the country had followed our lead, we wouldn't have had all these problems over all these years, either.[31]

In the twenty-first century the Republican Party could not afford a majority leader flying the flag of Jim Crow, and it cost Lott his newly won slot. But to say that senators who aspire to national leadership cannot fly Jim Crow's flag is not to say that Jim Crow has collapsed and its flag is dishonored. Roberts, a protégé of president Ronald Reagan, and just as smooth, "brilliantly" argued in his decision that just *because* of Jim Crow and slavery, the Court, if not the nation, must be scrupulous in surveying (let alone instantiating) its post-Jim Crow future. The chief justice recognized "non-recognition" of Jim Crow as the *principled* path for the Court to trudge in its decisions on public schools and the education of the nation's children. After all, he informed the country, in one pounce of a thought:

> The way to stop discrimination on the basis of race is to stop discriminating on the basis of race.[32]

At first I thought the chief justice was mimicking a tautology: "The way to do x is to do x."

Then I looked up *discrimination*:

> *Unfavorable treatment based on prejudice.*

Next I looked up *discriminating*:

Observing distinctions carefully; having good judgment.

Now, our chief justice is nothing if not one who observes distinctions carefully, so what is he telling the nation to do about its educational caste system? The way to stop unfavorable treatment based on prejudice is to stop observing carefully, making careful distinctions, and having good judgment on the basis of race?

Roberts became chief justice as a result of Mississippi's third plan for the nation, which Lott set in motion at the Neshoba County Fair of 1980, which he turned into Reagan's first stop on a duplicitous presidential path to "It's morning in America," a morning that made Roberts's day and opened his way. Trent Lott must be proud of John Roberts.[33]

Pity a nation whose jury pool of White and Black Jacksonians, thirty years after Medgar Evers's assassination, were almost universally ignorant of who he was, how he died, what his life meant for them; pity a nation whose chief justice thinks to make history by denying its relevance. Pity also Trent Lott who thinks that government has no business forcing one group of people to associate with another but has no idea whether that applied to Jim Crow. Lott left Mississippi for Washington in '68, to serve on the congressional staff of William Colmer, a Democrat, who decided to retire in '72; Lott won his open seat and in 1980 launched Ronald Reagan's post-convention presidential campaign at the Neshoba County Fair in Philadelphia, Mississippi, where Mickey Schwerner, Andrew Goodman, and James Chaney were lynched with the help of the sheriff.

The visual statement on television the next day was a sea of White faces at the Neshoba Fair with Reagan's words floating above them . . . he would reorder priorities and "restore to states and local governments the power that properly belongs to them."[34]

President Reagan, who had opposed both the Civil Rights Act and the Voting Rights Act, attracted the attention and became the personal hero of John Roberts, who joined the Reagan administration in 1981, where he worked to curtail all programs intended to bring minorities into settings where they were once shut out.

I was a college contemporary of Trent Lott's. When I was sitting in the Snick voter registration office in Greenwood on September 30, 1962, and Lott was a senior at Ole Miss, a pitched battle (the last) of the Redeemers and Governor Ross Barnet against U.S. marshals and

President Kennedy took place over the admission of James Meredith. In 1997, Senator Lott told *Time* magazine, "Yes, you could say that I favored segregation then. I don't know. The main thing was, I felt the federal government had no business sending in troops to tell the state what to do."[35]

Lucky for Lott, for the Redeemers and Reconcilers, and for the entire nation, the Snick-led insurgency, riding the currents of unpredictable terror, worked a strategy from 1961 to 1965 that dismantled Jim Crow in Mississippi without any federal troops, joining some and vacuuming others into a citizen's brigade that included civil rights organizations, college students, journalists, lawyers, doctors, judges, and the President and Attorney General of the United States. Did it all take place so Lott could boast at his press conference apologizing for flying Jim Crow's flag that Mississippi has more Black elected officials—897 as of July 2003—than any other state? What a difference that struggle has made to the state and the nation, and how quaint to have a chief justice who recognizes the "non-recognition" of Jim Crow as the foundation for the eradication of sharecropper education and the realization of the promise in the Fourteenth Amendment for national citizenship as constitutional people, but also how tragic. How tragic it is to have as the chief justice a supreme incarnation of President Reagan's inclination to walk into history and manipulate its presence.

Constitutional questions that attract and capture the attention of people all across the land do so because they accelerate into our personal lives. Whom shall we marry? With whom shall we school? These are constitutional questions about our common good: about the goods we distribute as a matter of course, a matter of history, and/or a matter of constitutional democracy. Such questions help us as a nation to reflect about the supreme law of the land and the evidence it assumes for the concepts it enshrines.

Presumably, Chief Justice Roberts had a concept to enshrine in his proclamation that to stop discriminating on the basis of race is the way to stop discrimination on the basis of race.[36]

But what kind of evidence are we to look for in assessing the usefulness of this concept as a guide into the promise of the Fourteenth Amendment to confer and withdraw fundamental rights tied to the nation's fate? Evidence of our failure as a nation to do so?

The nation might, perhaps, produce a president who can pick up where President Kennedy left off, when there was no solution in sight to such deep economic, social, and educational racial problems as those of the great cities where federal, state, and municipal policy in general coalesce, rather than clash. But President Kennedy was responding to the massive insurgency of the sit-ins and the civil rights movement.

We who are no longer constitutional property but not yet constitutional people have our work cut out for us. I take Amzie's ideal that one day the descendents of African slaves will become first-class citizens as the equivalent of our becoming constitutional people, and Amzie's theory and practice of a "race man" as a theory and practice not of the "adjudicated constitution" or the "legislated constitution," but the "lived constitution."[37] Let us use the Preamble to the Constitution as an organizing tool with which to assemble a twenty-first-century people's insurgency, for a substantive constitutional right to a quality public school education for every child in the nation.

In the eighteenth century we laid our constitution down with the concept of a constitutional person thick enough to obligate the federal government to track down IRS, insurgent runaway slaves, as constitutional property, to be shackled, and shipped to constitutional persons. In the twenty-first century we should pick our constitution up with the concept of a constitutional person thick enough to obligate the nation to secure for all its children a quality public school education as a matter of course, a matter of history, and a matter of our constitutional democracy.

"We the People" is an inescapable theoretical term in the Preamble. The Constitution could not begin, "We the President" or "We the Congress" or "We the Supreme Court." No, the Preamble locates itself as a force, not just among the citizens of the United States, but simply, without pretension, among its people. How could it have done otherwise? "We the people"—the Constitution—await its insurgents:

> We the people of the United States, in order to form a more perfect union, establish justice, insure domestic tranquility, provide for the common defense, promote the general welfare, and secure the blessings of liberty to ourselves and our prosperity, do ordain and establish this Constitution for the United States of America.

NOTES

1. Alfred W. Blumrosen and Ruth G. Blumrosen, *Slave Nation—How Slavery United the Colonies and Sparked the American Revolution* (Naperville, IL: Sourcebooks, 2005), chapter 1.
2. Ibid., 7.
3. Ibid., 10.
4. Ibid., 10.
5. Ibid., 11.
6. Ibid., 24.
7. The phrase is mine. It will help us to have an icon such as Somerset as part of our constitutional landscape.
8. Nicholas Lemann, *Redemption: The Last Battle of the Civil War* (New York: Farrar, Straus & Giroux, 2006), 185.
9. C. Vann Woodward, *The Strange Career of Jim Crow* (New York: Oxford University Press, 2000), 168–71.
10. Lemann, *Redemption*, 98.
11. Ibid., 98.
12. Ibid., 167.
13. Earl Black, *The Rise of Southern Republicans* (Cambridge, MA: Belknap Press of Harvard University Press, 2002), 44.
14. Susan Sontag, *At the Same Time: Essays and Speeches* (New York: Farrar, Straus, & Giroux, 2007), 215.
15. Lemann, *Redemption,* 179.
16. Ibid., 179–80.
17. Nicholas Lemann, *The Promised Land: The Great Black Migration and How It Changed America* (New York: Vintage Books, 1992), 51.
18. Maurice L. Risen, "Legal Aspects of Separation of Races in Public Schools" (PhD diss., Teachers College, Temple University, Philadelphia, PA, 1933), 2.
19. James Bryant Conant, *Slums and Suburbs: A Commentary on Schools in Metropolitan Areas* (New York: McGraw Hill, 1961), 8–11.
20. Woodward, *Strange Career,* 168–71.
21. Ibid.
22. Peter Berkowitz, "The Court, the Constitution and the Culture of Freedom," *Policy Review* (August–September 2005): 19,http://findarticles.com/p/articles/mi_qa3647/is_200508/ai_n14901581/pg_19.
23. David Lawrence, "Rights Law Brings Up Old Ratification Issue," *New York Herald Tribune,* July 6, 1964.
24. Burke Marshall, *Federalism and Civil Rights* (New York: Columbia University Press, 1964), 7.
25. John Doar, "Burke Marshall's Memorial," in *Yale Law School Journal* 113 (2004): 791–95.
26. Black, *Southern Republicans,* 44.
27. Editorial, "The Southern Delegations," *New York Times,* August 27, 1964.

28. U.S. Department of Justice, Voting Rights Act of 1965, http://www.usdoj
.gov/crt/voting/intro/intro_b.htm.

29. Lawrence, "Rights Law."

30. Laurence Tribe, quoted in "The Same Words, but Differing Views," by
Adam Liptak, *New York Times*, June 29, 2007.

31. Dan Goodgame and Karen Tumulty, "Tripped Up By History," *Time*,
December 23, 2002, http://www.time.com/time/magazine/article/0,9171,
1003912,00.html; Michael Kinsley, "Lott's Adventures in Gaffeland,"
Time, December 23, 2002, http://www.time.com/time/magazine/article/
0,9171,1003914,00.html; Karen Tumulty, "Trent Lott's Segregationist College Days," *Time Online/CNN*, December 12, 2002, http://www.time.com/
time/nation/article/0,8599,399310,00.html.

32. Linda Greenhouse, "Justices Limit the Use of Race in School Plans
for Integration," *New York Times*, June 29, 2007, http://www.nytimes
.com/2007/06/29/washington/29scotus.html?ex=1340769600&en=6db746
c138ff9893&ei=5088.

33. Joan Biskupic, "Roberts Steers Courts Right Back to Reagan," *USA Today*,
June 29, 2007, http://www.usatoday.com/news/washington/2007-06-28
-supreme-court-right_N.htm.

34. Black, *Southern Republicans*, 216–17.

35. Tumulty, "Lott's Segregationist College Days."

36. Greenhouse, "Justices."

37. Goodwin Liu introduces the concepts of the "adjudicated Constitution"
and the "legislated Constitution" in his writings: "Education, Equality,
and National Citizenship," *Yale Law Journal*, 116, no. 2, reprint (November
2006), and "Interstate Inequality in Educational Opportunity," *New York
University Law Review* 81, no. 6, reprint (December 2006), which led me
to use the phrase "lived Constitution" to describe the work of SNCC in
Mississippi in the '60s, when we worked in a context of Constitutional
permissiveness.

5

Quality Education as a Civil Right

Reflections

Ernesto Cortés Jr.

A good education is more than a civil right; it is the foundation necessary to sustain our democracy and modern civilization. Without the capacity to engage, question, argue, interpret, and contextualize experiences and encounters, authority is left unchallenged and individuals are left open to misdirection—which leaves them prey to the demagogues of hate. As Gerald Graff reminds us in *Clueless in Academe,* effective argument starts with attentive listening and understanding.[1] Real understanding and insight require not just a grasp of *what* was said, but also its context—the person's story, history, and experience. This kind of attentive listening leads to an understanding of differences and respect for others even in the midst of disagreement.

Historically we have learned these kinds of skills through our participation in institutions—congregations, schools, unions, settlement homes—which develop in us a deeper understanding of relationality and the value of engagement. Without the vibrancy of these institutions, our tendency is to withdraw into ourselves and revert to tribalism when confronted with that which is "other." This is a recipe for disaster in our increasingly polarized nation and globalized society. Given the diversity of culture, religion, economics, and politics, we must assume the existence of contradictions and embrace the tensions that they generate. Given that these differences cannot be eliminated, the question then becomes, How do we deal with them? Properly contextualized, argument and debate can be a substitute for violent conflict, which often leads to war.

Our impatience with the debate and negotiation that is part of the public decision-making process, coupled with our need for order, security, and decisiveness in times of crisis, can lead us all too quickly into an authoritarian, top-down culture in which we are assigned questions and told to answer. Now clearly in some contexts (the military, traffic lights, etc.) a culture of command and control is not only appropriate but necessary. However, this type of culture tends to reduce people and institutions to stereotypes, which may serve as useful categories for bureaucrats, marketers, and demagogues but don't lend themselves to the engagement that is necessary for real argument and negotiation.

Unfortunately, our institutions today, particularly our schools, reflect more and more the command and control model. They do not teach the culture of argument or the skills of deliberation. Yet to be an educated person is to understand that the subculture of argument undergirds all academic subjects. Assertions of truth or value in literature, art, history, science, math, or any other area are subject to debate, and, therefore, require the support of a well-reasoned argument. A well-reasoned argument is not the same as assault or mere contradiction. It is grounded in logic and context, and can sustain and respond to challenges.

As Dana Villa so cogently states in *Politics, Philosophy, Terror: Essays on the Thought of Hannah Arendt*, without the contestation inherent in an argument culture you are unlikely to recognize the limitations of your own.[2] Yet even the argument culture is not enough; to be well educated also requires the development of judgment. Neurological studies indicate that adolescents particularly have a limited capacity to make good judgments; that portion of the brain typically does not fully develop until the late teens/early twenties.[3] This makes the argument culture in schools all the more important. Adults have the obligation to reinforce and challenge what adolescents are learning, and to do that requires that they too be well versed in the argument culture.

Fortunately, the two are interconnected in that it is virtually impossible to develop good judgment without engaging in argument, because good judgment requires considering multiple points of view as well as understanding their contexts. Fully understanding someone's opinions requires an understanding of that person's story—the forces and pressures that have shaped his or her moral universe and worldview. To consider another's point of view is difficult unless you understand *why* someone believes what she believes, or why *you* believe what you believe. Often the first step is to know your own story. In the movie *Amistad,* Anthony Hopkins as John Quincy Adams makes the point that in all his experience in arguing before the Supreme Court he has learned that the person who tells the best story wins.[4] Logic and relevance are important, but storytelling is essential.

Contestation creates the possibility of an enlarged mentality and imagination. Properly conducted, it allows us to enter into one another's moral universes and understand the interconnectedness. Without it we become narrow, technical specialists who can do horrible things to one another because we do not consider the consequences. We engage in what Spanish-speakers refer to as *consificar*—to reduce someone to a mere part of themselves, or a thing.

Hannah Arendt reminds us of this possibility in her discussion of Adolf Eichmann. He was very smart, efficient, ambitious, and competent, but because he lacked an enlarged mentality, he was unable to consider fully the consequences of his monstrous attitudes and practices toward Jews, Gypsies, and homosexuals. He lacked the capacity to understand the humanity of his victims and defended his grotesque behavior as merely "following orders."[5] Evidence available today indicates that Eichmann was a more central player in the development of the Final Solution than originally acknowledged. This new evidence further reinforces the notion that he was literally unable to consider the fact that "other" people (non-Aryans) were a part of his moral universe.[6]

In contrast, Cornel West cites Herman Melville's capacity for an enlarged mentality as the genesis for the relationship between Ishmael and Queequeg, a man of color, in *Moby-Dick.* Melville's ability to imagine beyond the racial prejudices of his time in order to develop the storyline that depicts Queequeg as being more human than most god-fearing Christians clearly indicates not only the ability to get inside the story of the "other," but also the ability to imagine a context in which the limitations of his own time would be overcome by relationships and conversations.[7]

These examples suggest that a good education is more than literacy and numeracy; it equips people to be able to consider another's moral universe and recognize the common humanity that we all share. The real question of education should be how do we teach all of our institutions—not just our schools—to be attentive to the formation of people? Beyond educating and providing services and spiritual guidance, how do these institutions form people who understand the responsibilities of citizenship and what it means to be another's neighbor rather than just a member of our family, our clan, our tribe, or our community.

Perhaps these examples seem too esoteric for a discussion of the value of education. Yet I would assert that far too much of modern education, and indeed modern life, is about demanding answers to questions or solutions to problems, when often the real issue is overlooked. Rarely does anyone ask: Is this the right question? What's behind this question? Is it properly formulated, or have we rushed to judgment without considering all the factors? At the micro level, when our schools lack a well-developed culture of inquiry and argument, students learn to conduct searches on the Internet to find answers rather than puzzling through the relevance and dimensions of the questions being posed. On a larger scale I would suggest that without first grappling with the deeper question of why education is so crucial to the sustenance of modern civilization, we cannot begin to have a genuine debate about the details of what happens in our classrooms, on our campuses, and in our legislative bodies.

Our culture's emphasis on the answers at the expense of the questions is reflected in the narrowness of the vision of many of our schools. In most circumstances our schools don't draw on the intuitive ability of students to argue or persuade one another (or their parents). They don't build on the natural inquisitiveness of children by teaching them to form hypotheses and then test them. Instead, educators and administrators respond only to our natural desire for certainty and order. Today the tendency is to warehouse kids and bombard them with facts and figures—teaching "the truth" or "teaching to the test."

Our fear of uncertainty drives us to teach our students to live in intellectual, cultural, and political silos that leave no room for ambiguity, relationality, or engagement. From this perspective, everything is black or white/true or false in a binary world of artificially-constructed polarization, a mirror of our institutions, which seem intent on transmitting the existing culture, and consequently forget their role in cultivating human potential and preparing students for lives in a society undergoing constant change.

The desire for certainty and the unwillingness to embrace ambiguity in our culture have led to a system of education that is focused on instruction rather than teaching and on compliance rather than creativity. It ignores the role of teaching as a performing art, in which the practitioner must be entrepreneurial, creative, and willing to take risks.[8]

Real teaching and learning is based on the understanding that intellectual capital is more than merely information; it is the ability to analyze and reflect. We have to be prepared to teach students the wonder, awe, and beauty of the U.S. Constitution, while also recognizing it as a deeply flawed document that ignored women, propertyless men, and the horrors of slavery. Teaching should transmit the value of a culture while at the same time preparing students to challenge it and to learn from its shortcomings.

Education is also complicated because it does not occur in isolation from other issues. If children come to school hungry, sick, homeless, scared, or with uncorrected vision problems or if they come from homes warmed by high-sulfur heating oil or with inadequate sanitation systems, their education is compromised, if other institutions refuse to step in and address these life challenges. In his book *Class and Schools,* Richard Rothstein cites countless studies that document specific challenges to educational achievement, which are directly linked to socioeconomic status rather than to traditional education concerns. For example, he cites the fact that student mobility has been linked to academic performance and that 30 percent of the poorest children had attended at least three different schools by the third grade, in contrast to only 10 percent of middle-class children.[9]

In no way do I cite these factors as an excuse for public schools that are not achieving adequate standards of education. Rather, I intend to remind the reader that this is not the problem of a single institution, an individual, or even groups of individuals.

Moreover, mounting evidence indicates that the vast majority of children, regardless of wealth and income, spend increasing amounts of time with a growing force of electronic gadgets, televisions, computers, rather than in conversations with adults. These one-way systems of transmission might provide visual or auditory stimulation, but they do nothing to engage the child in practicing his or her own orality, which "provides the foundation for literacy."[10] That this is an issue for middle-class and upper-middle-class households as well as for poorer ones speaks to the sociological phenomenon of isolation and withdrawal referenced on the first page of this chapter.

Arendt makes the point in *Men in Dark Times* that human beings have an inclination in times of crisis to retreat into themselves, to seek the comfort of that which is familiar and similar, and to withdraw from public life. We become preoccupied with preservation and withdraw from the public square. While she does not criticize this survival instinct on its face, she wisely draws the connection of the power vacuum it leaves behind to the rise of demagogues who both prey on fears and anxieties and take advantage of the absence of participation in public life to create oppressive regimes. Specifically she cites this as a factor in the rise of the Third Reich in Weimar Germany.[11] I would submit that to the extent that we are not teaching the argument culture either in our schools or in our democracy as a whole, we are in fact reinforcing this dangerous inclination to withdraw from public life in "dark times."

The phenomenon becomes self-reinforcing in that schools do not prepare students to argue. When, as adults, they then withdraw from debate, this in turn creates a culture that does not value the very tradition on which democracy is based. There is no democratic culture without public education. As far back as the 1830s, free public education has been promoted as a "crucible of democracy, a blending of all children to function from a common set of values."[12] We have to understand that when we give up on public schools, we give up, at a minimum, on one of the most important pillars of democracy—and maybe on democracy itself.

Our commitment to a constitutional democracy is predicated on the belief that there will be conflict—conflict not only between the branches of government, but between groups of organized citizens, intermediate institutions, corporations, etc. The only question is how those conflicts will be resolved. The role of debate and argument is present throughout the system of democratic politics but is particularly embodied in the judiciary branch. The courts require a sophisticated culture of argument and contestation; judgment is rendered only after the consideration of the merits of the arguments of both contesting parties.

Daunting though it may seem, the Supreme Court of the United

States has given only one institution the charge to teach the habits and skills requisite for a democratic culture—the public school. Chief Justice Earl Warren clearly outlined the civic mission of the public schools in the Court's 1954 ruling:

> Today, education is perhaps the most important function of state and local governments. Compulsory school attendance laws and the great expenditures for education both demonstrate our recognition of the importance of education to our democratic society. It is required in the performance of our most basic public responsibilities, even service in the armed forces. It is the very foundation of good citizenship.[13]

However, it was never intended that the schools perform this task alone, but rather that they were embedded in a network of overlapping institutions such as churches, synagogues, settlement homes, unions, neighborhood associations, lodges, clubs, and mutual aid societies. The assumption was that the mutual engagement of the public schools with all these institutions would underpin what we now call civil society.

It is in these networks of institutions that adults developed the skills of attentive listening and understanding that undergird the culture of argument and deliberation. It is in these kinds of conversations that people get to know one another's story and thereby develop a deeper understanding of alternative points of view. In the early 1980s, for example, when the Texas Industrial Areas Foundation (IAF) Network was organizing to support a new education finance and accountability system, one of the biggest stumbling blocks for the network was the issue of funding for bilingual education. Members of some of the more middle-class Anglo congregations involved in the network thought bilingual education was a strategy that kept students from learning English and becoming "more American." It was only through conversations and engagement (twenty-seven small group meetings in one congregation alone) with those who had experiences different from their own that a common understanding emerged. The respectful contestation that resulted in the emergence of that common understanding made the congregations ready allies to fight with the parents and the schools to fully fund bilingual education.[14]

Frequently even the relationships inside schools benefit from the engagement with networks of other institutions. Robert Cordova, principal of Harmony Elementary in the Los Angeles Unified School District, initially saw his work with the congregations and unions of One-LA IAF as a way to deflect the concerns of parents onto different institutions. However, once Cordova began to have conversations with and be mentored by other institutional leaders in his community, he began to see himself not just as a manager of crises, but as an educational leader in a network of institutions with a broader vision for the transformation of his school and community. He began to see the benefit of working with people outside the walls of his campus and started thinking of parents as assets rather than liabilities. Today, parents hold positions of responsibility on the campus's core leadership team alongside educators and classified employees. Harmony has also begun organizing Achievement Academies to identify and develop additional parent leaders, as well as equipping them with the academic content knowledge necessary to participate more fully in their children's education.

The attention of One LA-IAF to this type of transformation grew in part from similar relationships forged on campuses working with the Texas IAF network throughout the state. In just one example, teachers and parents developed new relationships at Zavala Elementary in Austin in a context that, on the face of it, appeared to have little to do with education. In 1991, a meeting between Zavala parents and teachers about test scores and student achievement had reduced teachers to tears. Parents were angry; teachers felt attacked. Through individual conversations with parents and teachers, organizers with Austin Interfaith (the local IAF affiliate) uncovered a common concern: health care for the students.[15] Teachers identified poor health conditions as one of the factors related to student achievement; parents mentioned the two- month waiting period at the local clinic as their first concern. When the city announced that the clinic would be closed for the removal of asbestos and mold, organizers posed the question: Why not provide immunizations and other basic preventive services for students on the campus itself?

More than two hundred parents and teachers came together to strategize about the possibility. For many it was the first time they had witnessed both sides working toward a common, concrete goal.

The health department agreed to the proposal, but the school board hesitated in the face of a vocal minority from outside the school community who raised the question of whether school-based health services opened the door for reproductive health services (condoms for kindergarteners!). At a December school board meeting, sixty parents and twenty teachers stayed well into the night to testify on behalf of their common agenda. Leaders from Austin Interfaith's religious institutions spoke in favor of the proposal as well. The board's favorable vote was unanimous.

Parents and teachers at Zavala had been transformed through their engagement with one another and their common struggle to secure health care for their children. They went on to organize a new curriculum for the campus, creative after-school programs, and a science-intensive program designed to help students achieve admission to a science magnet junior high school, where only one Zavala student had achieved admission in the previous ten years. The Young Scientists' Program was particularly noteworthy because, despite the fact that only a minority of the campus's fifth-grade students would directly benefit, hundreds of teachers, parents, and other Austin Interfaith leaders made the case before the school program and, ultimately, secured members' support.

These three examples highlight the potentially transformative nature of relationships between schools and other community institutions, the networks of which have produced well-documented improvements in academic achievement, teacher morale, and so forth.[16] At their best, these networks of institutions are developed into broad-based constituencies which also support the tax increases and bond elections necessary for investments in public education more broadly. To the extent that they remain focused on more traditional kinds of support for public schools—guest speakers, volunteers, and fund-raising events—the unintended consequences of these relationships are that their voluntary dimensions allow us to indulge in the belief that public education can be sustained on the cheap. This belief was further reinforced by the fact that, until recent decades, the public schools had a virtually captive labor market from which to draw.

Gender discrimination meant that teaching was one of the few professional paid-employment options widely available to women. In short, it was a buyer's market, and schools benefited by being able to pay relatively low wages to dedicated teachers. Fortunately for women, those labor market conditions have changed, providing a wide range of opportunities for educated professionals. Unfortunately, public schools have not had the resources to respond to the change in market conditions by increasing salaries and benefits in this more competitive labor market.

At the same time, the rise of the high-stakes testing regime has robbed teachers of much of the power to determine what goes on inside their classrooms and on their campuses. This hierarchical system does not value the collegiality and mentoring relationships that are central to the social dimensions of teaching.

Recent decades have also witnessed the deterioration of the relationships among schools and the other mediating institutions in their neighborhoods and communities. The mediating institutions themselves have experienced a decline as economic pressures have forced adults to work longer hours, leaving less time for voluntary associations. At the same time, the testing regime has left teachers and principals with less time and energy to invest in relationships outside the campus. The absence of these relationships—of an external constituency that cares about the success of the school—leaves the campuses short of both human capital and the financial capital generated by taxpayers demanding a greater investment in public education.

Given the demands of a twenty-first-century economy and a growing population of Social Security recipients, it is in our national self-interest to invest in education and to educate all children. There has always been a debate about who should be educated in America. Thomas Jefferson's proposal for a public school system in Virginia excluded women, slaves, and farmers. Of course, Jefferson's commitment to maintaining a small, agrarian economic system didn't require the economic growth fueled by universal education. As America's leaders began to recognize both the potential and the challenge of a much more diversified economy, education took on more significance. By the 1840s, Henry Clay's American System required expanding investments not only in infrastructure throughout the nation, but in education as well.[17] As the manufacturing industry was fueled by the Civil War, the westward expansion, and the emerging Common Market, the demand for immigrant workers increased and the need for a universal common school became self-evident.

Today a small but vocal minority argues that the children of un-documented immigrants should be excluded from our school systems, just as they argued against educating African Americans, Catholics, and a host of other minorities throughout the history of the United States. From an economic perspective alone, it is in our self-interest to educate children regardless of whether their parents have papers. Countless studies have documented that a well-educated workforce earns higher wages, pays higher taxes, requires fewer government services, and generates economic growth through both production and consumption.

Notwithstanding its value in preparing an educated workforce, the real reason taxpayers should support public education is its role in the value and vision of a democratic culture. Only if education is about teaching people—particularly young people—to understand other perspectives and points of view while maintaining the ability to debate and argue their own can we hope to sustain democracy in the face of the growing isolationism, cynicism, and polarization not just in our own nation, but also in the global community.

That our Constitution exists implies a right to an education; why guarantee a set of rights and liberties unless you presuppose that citizens will be sufficiently well-educated to understand them? President Ulysses S. Grant understood this when he encouraged Congress to pass a constitutional amendment guaranteeing a free quality public education to every child in the United States in 1875. His claim that "free public education lay at the root of the nation's liberty" clearly indicates his belief that education is a prerequisite to freedom.[18] The fact that the language of his proposed amendment created the right to an education for "all children, irrespective of sex, color, birthplace or religion" is a reminder of the lessons he drew from the institution of slavery, the Civil War, and Reconstruction: as a nation we are inevitably interconnected.[19] Or, as Benjamin Franklin so adroitly stated: "We can all hang together or we can all hang separately."[20]

If democracy is to last, we must also learn reverence—which means we value something beyond ourselves and our bank accounts. It means we understand and value responsibility, obligation, duty, and a consideration of long-term horizons. Reverence reflects the public piety of Emerson and Whitman when we recognize our economic, social, and spiritual debts to those who have gone before. It requires courage and imagination and a realization that the self emerges only in relationship with others, with an understanding of the different cultural contexts of ourselves and our neighbors. Otherwise, we are at risk of producing a nation of people who are too imprisoned by their fears and anxieties, by their needs and necessities, by the culture of consumption, to have any sense of reverence at all. This is surely a path to destruction. While we search the globe for monsters to destroy in the name of exporting democracy, we should sustain it here at home.

NOTES

1. Gerald Graff, *Clueless in Academe* (New Haven, CT: Yale University Press, 2003), 2.
2. Dana R. Villa, *Politics, Philosophy, Terror: Essays on the Thought of Hannah Arendt* (Princeton, NJ: Princeton University Press, 1999), 124–25.
3. Lee Bowman, "New Research Shows Stark Differences in Teen Brains," *Scripps Howard News Service,* May 11, 2004, http://www.deathpenaltyinfo .org/new-research-shows-stark-differences-teen-brains.
4. David Franzon, *Amistad* (Hollywood, CA: Dreamworks Video, 1997).
5. Villa, *Politics, Philosophy, Terror,* 45.
6. Christopher Browning, *The Origins of the Final Solution: The Evolution of Nazi Jewish Policy, September 1939–March 1942* (Lincoln: University of Nebraska Press, 2004), 37-43.David Cesarini, *Becoming Eichmann: Rethinking the Life, Crimes, and Trial of a "Desk Murderer"* (Cambridge, MA: Da Capo Press, 2007), 117–58.
7. Cornel West, *Democracy Matters* (New York: Penguin Press, 2004), 89.
8. Seymour Sarason, *Teaching as a Performing Art* (New York: Teachers College, Columbia University, 1999), 6.
9. Richard Rothstein, *Class and Schools* (Washington, D.C.: Economic Policy Institute, 2004), 46.
10. Barry Sanders, *A Is for Ox: The Collapse of Literacy and the Rise of Violence in an Electronic Age* (New York: Vintage Books, Random House, 1994), 4.
11. Jeffrey C. Isaac, *Democracy and Dark Times* (Ithaca, NY: Cornell University Press, 1998), 24.
12. Robert H. Wiebe, *The Opening of American Society* (New York: Alfred A. Knopf, 1984), 309.
13. Supreme Court of the United States, *Brown v. Board of Education* (347 U.S. 483), 3.
14. Dennis Shirley, *Community Organizing for Urban School Reform* (Austin: University of Texas Press, 1997), and *Valley Interfaith and School Reform: Organizing for Power on South Texas* (same publisher, 2001).

15. Eva Gold, Elaine Simon, and Chris Brown, "Case Study: Austin Interfaith," in *Strong Neighborhoods, Strong Schools: Successful Community Organizing for School Reform* (Chicago: Cross City Campaign for Urban School Reform, March 2002), 42.

16. Thomas Hatch, "How Community Contributes to Achievement," *Educational Leadership* 55(8): 1998, 15-16.Richard Murnane and Frank Levy, "The First Principle: Agree on the Problem," in *Teaching the New Basic Skills: Principles for Educating Children to Thrive in a Changing Economy* (New York: The Free Press, 1996), 80-108.

17. Wiebe, *Opening of American Society*, 308.

18. Jean Edward Smith, *Grant* (New York: Touchstone, Simon & Schuster, 2001), 569.

19. Ibid., 570.

20. Jared Sparks, *The Life of Benjamin Franklin: Containing the Autobiography, with Notes and a Continuation* (Boston: Whittemore, Niles and Hall, 1856), 408.

PART III

Pursuing Excellence in a Context of Inequities

6

Stepping Stories

Creating an African American Community of Readers

Kimberly N. Parker

My grandmother told me, when I was young, that I should consider teaching; she felt I was bossy enough for it, and I was so passionate about reading that it would be something to share with others. Growing up on a small farm on the outskirts of Lexington, Kentucky, however, I had other dreams. I wanted to attend college and then pursue a law career. A semester at Colby College in Waterville, Maine, quickly steered me toward being an English major, as I became enthralled with literature and talking about books and great writing.

Several years after I graduated from Colby, I finally listened to my grandmother's advice. I went to Boston College for my masters in education and began teaching at a charter school, Codman Academy Charter School, full of all those aspirations and ideas new teachers have, but with really no concept of what to expect.

My first class of thirty-five students was comprised entirely of students of African American, Haitian American, Puerto Rican, and Caribbean American descent. The majority were being raised by a single mother. The parents, though busy, came to school for conferences and spoke to me regularly over the phone about their children's progress.

The school's mission was to use a college preparatory curriculum to prepare students for academic success. All of its students would be the first in their families to attend college. The school utilized the approach of looping, in which I followed this group of students through their freshman and sophomore years, allowing plenty of time for familiarity and community building. All classes were full inclusion, meaning my class had a significant percentage of students with special needs (about 25 percent). As a charter school teacher, I had tremendous flexibility to design and implement my own curriculum (both exciting and dangerous for a new teacher), as long as it was aligned with the Massachusetts state standards and National Council of Teachers of English standards. Creating a community of readers and writers was the cornerstone of my teaching. I knew how important reading was in my own life, how a good book could stay with me for days, and how exciting it was to talk to someone about reading. My students, however, did not enter my class with those same experiences. In early reading surveys I conducted at the beginning of their freshman year, many described their experiences with reading as "Reading sucks"; "I hate reading"; "I've never read a book, and I don't intend to start now." From the very first week, the gauntlet was thrown.

What I hoped to accomplish with these students was to create an "intentional community" of achievement. In such a community, they would learn to see themselves as academic achievers. I would set the academic bar extremely high, then carefully structure my classroom to ensure they had the support necessary to experience academic success. Theresa Perry in *Young, Gifted and Black: Promoting High Achievement Among African-American Students,* argues that Black students need to create what she calls a "counternarrative." According to Perry, the purpose of the counternarrative is to confirm the "collective identity of African Americans as literate, achieving people."[1] Traditionally, students of color have been perceived by larger society as incapable of achieving academic success. However, Perry asserts that

> African-American students will achieve in school environments that have a leveling culture, a culture of achievement that extends to all of its members and a strong sense of group membership, where the expectation that everyone achieve is explicit and is regularly communicated in public and group settings.[2]

Furthermore, this "creates an identity for African Americans, as individuals and as a people, that is not only not at odds with but coincident with intellectual achievement."[3] The rest of this chapter details the development of this community and my attempts to help my students create their own counternarrative.

YEAR ONE: EARLY STAGES OF
THE INTENTIONAL COMMUNITY

As I prepared for that first year, I was guided by the words of the principal in my former school, a Massachusetts Teacher of the Year, who told me to "win the kids over, then work the hell out of them." Figuring out exactly how to do this would drive the curriculum decisions I made. A colleague at the charter school told me my students would be below grade level academically. And, he added, because the charter school drew from public schools throughout Boston, they would have wildly varying levels of achievement. This was confirmed during those first weeks; I assigned a reading survey and some short writing diagnostics as homework. I received only a couple back. A few students told me that they did not do homework. Since their middle schools did not assign it, homework was a foreign concept for them.

In determining my curriculum, I was also guided by my own academic experience. I had always done well academically in a challenging environment. I had a good idea what it took to ensure academic success. However, I was unsure how to convey this reality to students who were unfamiliar with the amount of work it involved. That said, I decided to adopt a policy of setting the bar high. With that as a standard, I hoped to teach students the skills necessary to complete a high-quality task, reflect on the process, then move to the next task. Of course, this would involve considerable buy-in from the students.

While I envisioned a classroom of students actively engaged in their learning and focused on authentic assignments and products as ultimate goals, my more simple, immediate goal was to start them reading. I knew that for every task I wanted them to accomplish, I would have to explicitly teach them how to accomplish the task, articulating expectations and making the necessary corrections along the way.

My students were underachievers. There were enough students with such strong, off-putting personalities (with crossed arms, rolling eyes, and loud sighs, their entire affects screaming "leave me alone") that I could see how previous teachers rewarded them for being quiet. These were the students, however, that I found to be the most creative and open to suggestions. They were also the ones with whom I made some of my biggest new teacher mistakes (reading a student's body language incorrectly, not allowing a student to save face in front of his/her peers) but learned the best lessons about teaching and human behavior. The majority of these students were quite comfortable with worksheets, but when challenged with open-ended questions, they froze, attempted to derail the class with off-task behavior, or simply shut down completely.

During those early days, I relied increasingly on interpreting what students were not saying. My classes were two and a half hours during the first year (in the sophomore year, class time increased to three hours), which was conducive to activities that lent themselves to improvement over time. Relying on the reading and writing workshop model that stressed minilessons and then time for students to work on tasks, we would practice skills required to interact with peers (such as how to ask follow-up questions in a conversation and how to listen, even when someone had a differing opinion), and then I would circulate around the class. It was then that I learned what students were interested in when they were not in class, the music to which they listened, the places they went, the people whom they knew. I then incorporated their experiences and needs into my curriculum as much as possible.

I constantly worked to counter students' images of athletes with ones of African American poets, doctors, lawyers, and teachers. Exposing them to these different people, via field trips and classroom visitors, as well as newspaper articles and read-alouds, helped them consider a future beyond the playground. I wanted my students to read classic literature, and I wanted them to read literature from people who looked like them. I knew that for every text I selected and every decision I made, I would need to guide students through the process. Much of this involved simply showing them how to produce high quality work (which involved a lot of late nights at home constructing my own models of what I considered an "A" project or paper), as they had never seen it before; for what they envisioned as high quality work was woefully inadequate for my classroom.

I always arrived at school in enough time to run early-morning study halls and was rewarded with students who showed up regularly to work with me either alone or in small groups. During these times, I reinforced skills, clarified instruction, and got to know my students. Sometimes, they did not need my help at all; they would come in, arrange their possessions, and read silently or work on an assignment. It was as if they simply needed the reassurance that I was nearby should anything occur.

The first major project I assigned my students in their freshman year was to write a prehistoric short story of eight to ten pages. The school combined English and history. I decided to start with the dawn of the age of man and work our way forward. After building their background knowledge through short lectures, I laid out the project. We would use the weeks and months leading up to the final short story due in early December to work through multiple drafts of their stories.

When I handed out the assignment, more than one student muttered to her peers that I was crazy. At this point in the first semester, the longest assignment I had had them write was about a page. Now, eight pages! I responded, "I will not set you up to fail. I know you can do this work, and I'm not going to give up on you." Yes, more eyes rolled and profanity was whispered under breaths. In the back of my head, I wondered if, indeed, I *was* crazy. I knew it was going to require a LOT of work on my part—not only the final grading, but the minilessons around issues of craft, the structure of a short story, the revisions—but I knew they could do it.

And so, we worked. Every day, framed by a minilesson, we worked on the craft of writing short stories. We talked about characters and setting. I made checklists. We brainstormed characteristics of prehistory and discussed how to integrate them into stories. I set due dates for drafts and revisions and hounded those students who were reluctant, those who got stuck, and those who had fantastic ideas but little command of language.

One young man created a hero named Acka Packa who was out on a hunt for food and met the love of his life. He could describe the story and the smallest details excellently, but, when it came time for him to write the story, he simply could not do it. Finally, he dictated the story to another teacher, who typed it for him. It was a constant dance of figuring out what they needed based on what I observed, what I overheard, what I wanted.

As the weeks passed, students began to give names to their characters, defend their choice of conflicts, and revise their writing. When the project concluded, most of my students turned in a final draft, and we celebrated with a Publishing Party. While I had hoped for every student to turn in a final draft, some students simply refused. This struck a blow to my attempts to create community. All students who turned in a story, though, were invited to share cake and snacks with our community of writers. This party did more than any of my chastising and goading because they discussed how exciting and fun it was to talk about their stories with guests and their friends. The students who did not attend the Publishing Party vowed to attend the next one; and, for the most part, they did. In their reflections (a staple of any work we did), students voiced what would become a common sentiment about their work: "I didn't know I could create this sort of work. I am proud of what I did."

THE *ODYSSEY*

Armed with the short story success, we moved on. I wanted to integrate reading and writing even more, and, using Homer's *Odyssey*, I was able to do this. I selected Robert Fitzgerald's translation because it was lyrical and accessible. I knew the epic would be difficult for students, and to create multiple points of entry, I rounded up a number of picture books and began most days with a read-aloud. Students were also able to read these books at their leisure. I expected varying amounts of success with reading the text because they still were not confident readers. Sure enough, students expressed admiration for Odysseus and skepticism at Penelope's loyalty. This was an entry point into the story.

But, for many of them, the strongest connection came with Odysseus's son, Telemachus. For a number of people in the classroom, myself included, an absentee father was not a foreign concept. Many days, we debated what Telemachus should do and what students would have done in those same circumstances. Some wanted Telemachus to give up and move on, to believe that his father was never coming back, while others thought that he did what a son was supposed to do: wait for his father. Upon concluding the reading, I told students that I selected this book because I knew they were ready for it—again, I was met by smirks of disbelief. Their reaction quickly changed when I told them that the *Odyssey* was usually reserved for upper-level honors English classes elsewhere in the city. I mentioned it in passing, moving on to another task. Sure enough, students turned to each other, smiling, as they appreciated their accomplishment.

The writing task that accompanied reading the *Odyssey* was to create a collaborative community epic.[4] Students would create their own hero and decide from where he was returning (both classes selected the Gulf War); then each student would be responsible for writing a chapter about the hero's experiences in a given part of the world. Operating within the workshop, students moved through the writing cycle, consulting with each other, writing their chapters, and compiling the final work.

Throughout the remainder of that school year, I relied on making sure students could always have a piece of quality work of which they could be proud. Work was displayed and talked about, and they kept working portfolios. Slowly but surely, students' academic self-perceptions were changing. I was working behind the scenes as well to make sure they were experiencing success. I called home every week to talk to them and their parents. I sent home weekly newsletters that celebrated our community progress. I took any opportunity I could create to applaud my students and the academic stars they were becoming, even recognizing those students who were working hard as "Students of the Week."

OUTSIDE READING

In addition to reading shared texts, students had a standing assignment to complete thirty minutes of reading outside class. For the most part, they followed the requirement. They wrote weekly book logs, which I used to gauge what they were reading (and whether they were reading). Students were permitted to read any text of their choice during these independent sessions, and often they checked out books from our classroom library. Initially, I experienced some trepidation in lending out books to students, as many of the selections within the library were my own books I had acquired over the years and that I loved dearly. I spoke often about my love for those books, as well as others in the library, and how not returning them would put everyone in the classroom at a disadvantage. Over those two years, out of over five hundred titles in the library, only five were never returned, and the students who had those books arranged to pay for them before the school year ended. Our reading area had some rocking chairs, floor pillows, and a couch. Students were free to sit where they liked as long as they were reading.

PEER PRESSURE

One of the advantages of teaching within a small school was that my students spent a lot of time with me and with each other. As a result, peer groups influenced many social interactions. This was another key element of building an intentional community: the need to influence the peer group rather than just the individual. That first year, I had more boys in my class (and even more the following year as sophomores). I knew that, for the most part, the boys did not consider themselves readers, but I also knew, from talking to their parents, that some of them were "closet readers"; they read at home, in the privacy of their rooms, but never talked about it.

Prior to the start of that school year, I found a series of books written by Sharon Draper: *Tears of a Tiger, Darkness Before Dawn,* and *Forged By Fire.* The trilogy centered on a group of African American urban high school students affected by the death of one of their friends, a basketball player. Nearly all of my male students obsessed about basketball; nearly half of them believed they could play basketball professionally.

One day, as I moved through the classroom, I casually mentioned to Travis, the captain of our basketball team, that I had a book that he might want to read. I singled him out deliberately; Travis had tremendous social capital among his peers. They followed him faithfully. He asked me about the book, and I said it was "about some kids who play basketball and one dies." I made another circuit around the room and returned to drop the book on his table. Travis was indifferent about reading; he had dyslexia, which complicated his reading and frustrated him to no end. Over the last couple of years, he had fallen into a habit of not reading much. For a few moments, Travis stared at the cover of the book, which pictured a teenage African American boy. He turned it over and read the back, as I had instructed students to do in earlier minilessons about selecting books. Opening it, he read the first chapter and was captivated instantly.

The book begins immediately with action—a newspaper report details the death of a star high school basketball player. Travis was hooked. Students read every day for fifteen to twenty minutes in a program called Sustained Silent Reading (SSR). That day, when SSR wound down, he asked if he could take the book home with him, and I consented. The following day, he raised his hand and asked, in a loud voice, if we could have a "Book Talk" because his book was "hot." During Book Talks, students describe a book they are reading. It is a great way to get students to read books they might not other-wise know anything about. An endorsement by a peer carried much more weight than an endorsement by me. Travis was so excited and enthusiastic that I relented. After he spoke, providing a plot summary and some editorializing about the characters and predictions about their motivations, two other boys, Demetrius and John, perked up. Demetrius immediately declared that he wanted to read the book af-ter Travis. John, not wanting to be left out, echoed the same desire.

Two days later, Travis completed *Tears of a Tiger* and moved on to the second book. Demetrius finished *Tears of a Tiger* in a day, gave it to John, and waited impatiently for Travis to move through the tril-ogy. I had these three boys in my homeroom, and they talked inces-santly about the books. I, of course, added my own opinions, and thus began to transition them into a culture of readers.

This group of boys had tremendous influence over the rest of their peers. Travis was a natural leader; he was funny, worked hard, and collaborated well. Whenever groups formed, everyone wanted to be in his. They were not put off by his difficulty reading and writing. In fact, they often pitched in to help him. Travis, in turn, would guide the groups but was also excellent at involving others. Throughout that freshman year, the boys shared books with each other, talked about books in small groups, and, most importantly, slowly began to consider themselves true readers.

READING RESOURCES

My graduate school training had not prepared me to provide explicit reading instruction, something my students really needed. I sought numerous resources and, near the end of that first year, found the best ones to be by Stephanie Harvey (*Strategies that Work*) and Kylene Beers (*When Kids Can't Read and What Teachers Can Do*). What guided me the most was the belief that students become better readers by reading. I was relentless in my quest to get the right books into their hands. I scoured local used bookstores and yard sales for books my students might be interested in reading. I was able to stock my classroom library with a large selection of African American titles of interest. Increasingly, students relied less on my suggestions and began to trust themselves and each other more. I talked so much about my own reading, about what made a book "good" for me and what made me "abandon titles" (stop reading), that I think students came to realize that reading was just something good students did. And, since I was so convinced that they were the smartest students on the earth, then it made sense for them to internalize those beliefs as well. Midway through their freshman year, students ceased to argue when I told them it was time for SSR, and instead, at the end of those sessions, more and more students would request "five more minutes" to finish their page or chapter.

In the meantime, we read Shakespeare's *Romeo and Juliet* and Lee's *To Kill a Mockingbird*. Our reading of *Mockingbird* was framed in the context of Jim Crow segregation in the South. My students were unfamiliar with the history of African Americans in the United States, something that alarmed and disappointed me; after all, my grandparents had made it a point of pride for me to learn my own history. I harped on making sure they took every possible opportunity to learn their history. We studied the case of the Scottsboro Boys before reading *Mockingbird*. I would use this desire for students to learn their history to ground much of my curriculum the following year.

At the end of my students' freshman year, I was confident I had laid the foundation for their sophomore experience. In their end-of-year evaluations, all of them said they realized they were capable of doing good work and that they had surprised even themselves with their personal achievement.

SUMMER ACTIVITIES

That summer, I worked with a group of six boys who needed a few weeks longer to reach the passing mark (a C). Every day, we read and worked on writing skills. We also took trips to the neighborhood library. Essentially, it was a book club that lasted for three weeks. During that time I realized how cohesive this group of boys was (Travis was in it, coincidentally). I spoke to my principal about teaching one section of boys the following year because this one group had such powerful chemistry (the entire sophomore class was thirteen boys and six girls). She agreed, and those six boys became the foundation for a same-sex class that would stabilize at ten boys.

Over the summer, I continued to read about adolescent literacy and made plans to raise my already high standards. After attending a literacy conference hosted by Expeditionary Learning and receiving Harvey Daniels's *Literature Circles: Voice and Choice in Book Clubs and Reading* Groups, I decided that I would make Literature Circles the cornerstone of my curriculum.

YEAR TWO: LITERATURE CIRCLES

That fall, after explicitly teaching students reading strategies, we started with a rereading of *To Kill a Mockingbird*. My students had never experienced reading a text for a second time. Of course, they grumbled, but those same students later acknowledged how much they missed the first time (as well as how much they had not read or did not understand). While we reread the novel, I trained students in the procedures of Literature Circles. They practiced finding compelling passages to discuss, writing reading logs, and asking questions to keep their discussions going.

Sufficiently satisfied that they knew enough to participate in their own Literature Circles, students spent the next month reading such selections as *A Lesson Before Dying, Warriors Don't Cry, The Secret Life of Bees,* and *The Adventures of Tom Sawyer,* among others. Later, after students complained, I integrated more young adult literature and nonfiction.

To participate in these discussions, students had to first complete an elaborate set of notes. They were required to find passages to discuss, take notes on the plot, make connections to their lives and draw a picture that captured some part of what they were reading. The notes had to be complete in order to receive a stamp for credit (which would later be part of their grades). In the early going, there were quite a few notes I did not stamp. Students were expected to fill up an entire page with required material, and if they were even the smallest bit incomplete, they did not receive credit. I needed to do this only a few times, however, before students began to take responsibility and complete the notes. And, more importantly, they were doing this outside of class.

The connections that they made and discussions they conducted were quite stilted at first: talking about books in a meaningful way was a new concept for them. They had to say more than "I liked it" or "I thought it was boring." The minilessons that accompanied Literature Circles focused on expanding discussion topics and digging deeper into the text. I modeled my own thinking about what I was reading and attempted to make the classroom a safe space where it was acceptable to argue about a title or passionately express feelings about books. The most tangible evidence of this comfort came when one day, during a discussion of *Tom Sawyer*, one of the boys enthusiastically exclaimed to his group, "Man, I like Tom Sawyer. He's tricky. He's like the Odysseus of the South!"

ESSAY WRITING AND READING
OUTSIDE OF THE CLASSROOM

The Literature Circles were not the only outside assignments for which students were responsible. Because of their weak writing skills, I required students to write a weekly five-paragraph essay that had to be of the correct length (eight to ten sentences per paragraph) and typed. We focused on the five-paragraph essay because it was mandated by the MCAS administered in the spring of the sophomore year. I stressed the need for "formal English" in their writing. I instructed them to never assume that the audience for whom they were writing knew them or knew about their experiences. We had several conversations about the need to "switch" language for the appropriate occasion. I was candid about the necessity of using different languages for given situations, sharing my own experiences and letting them know they would have to do the same thing: to succeed in mainstream society, they would need to know and practice the rules of standard English.

Over the course of the year, students completed an average of 95 percent of their essays. The move toward writing essays was difficult for students, since I had previously encouraged them to develop their individual voices. Now I wanted them to write formally. Their writing and my instruction became much more focused on "writing for the test."

Students who had trouble organizing worked first from templates, mastering the smaller parts of an essay and understanding how it fit into the larger overall context. This hard work paid off, as my students all passed the MCAS, and 77 percent scored in the Proficient and Advanced categories.

Students were always expected to be reading independently, a practice begun in the freshman year. I also wanted to capitalize on the progress the boys experienced in summer school. Journalist Darcy Frey had updated his compelling book, *The Last Shot: City Streets, Basketball Dreams,* which focused on high school basketball and the harsh reality of how very few players who dream of "making it" professionally ever do.

I pulled Travis aside and told him that I wanted to start a "secret society," strictly for sophomore boys. I said I needed his help in selecting group members who would be willing to meet after school and do the reading in addition to their other in-school work. I gave him a brief synopsis of *The Last Shot,* purposefully being vague on details, but inserting enough description to pique his interest. He whispered the names of ten boys in my ear. After class, I made them the same offer. All accepted and agreed to stop by after school to pick up their books.

The boys created their own reading schedule, reading about two to three chapters for each meeting, and meeting once a week. I supplied snacks. Occasionally, they chipped in to buy pizza. During our first meeting, it became clear that the group divided between boys who had begun reading (Travis was one of those) and ones who were attracted by the secrecy of the group but were not committed to doing the required reading. The boys decided that attendance was determined by reading; if a boy had not completed the reading, then he was not allowed to attend. They followed that rule for all of their meetings.

Six regular members were in the final group that continued to meet throughout the semester. The boys connected deeply to Frey's book, with little to no prodding from me. At one meeting, I asked how the reality portrayed in the book affected their lives. Travis said that he wanted to play basketball for Duke, but he wanted to be a lawyer as well. Antwan, too, wanted a professional basketball career, but his "backup plan" included acting and a possible stint as a lawyer. This was the first time these young men had articulated any desire to pursue any career other than professional sports.

Membership in the boys' book club—known as BBF (Black Boys are Fabulous)—was worn like a badge of honor. Members guarded their books, marked passages and questions with sticky notes, reminded me that it was time for a discussion, grumbled when I had to postpone a scheduled meeting. The boys even met informally on their own! The success the boys experienced in the afterschool book club affected their in-school work. The connections they made between what they were reading improved. They asked higher-order thinking questions more; they talked about books and reading in the halls and during lunch. There was a sense of pride about being a member in the group.

POEMS/SHAKESPEARE

In addition to the Literature Circles and the test-writing, students regularly memorized and recited poems and soliloquies from plays. As freshmen, students memorized "Invictus" by William Ernest Henley. Consequently, they would walk around school whispering to themselves, "I am the master of my fate. I am the captain of my soul." I often chanted this line to them, on days when they felt their most despondent: either they had not scored as well as hoped on an assignment or they were besieged by teen angst in some form. Other recitations included "Dreams" by Langston Hughes and "Nothing Gold Can Stay" by Robert Frost. During the time before a recitation, students would coach each other through the poems. They cheered for their classmates on the day of recitations.

In the spring of their sophomore year, students memorized Macbeth's soliloquy "Tomorrow and tomorrow and tomorrow" and delivered it, in unison, at a school-wide Renaissance fair. It was one of the most thrilling moments I have experienced as a teacher; to have twenty students reciting Macbeth's powerful words, in complete understanding of the text.

We did a lot of work with Shakespeare. I knew students were afraid of reading his plays; I had had my own difficulties with it as a student and a teacher. We read *Romeo and Juliet* as freshmen and *Macbeth* as sophomores. Each time, we focused on getting past the language by playing games and rewriting sections of the text as well as acting out as much as we could. Students were captivated by the relationship between the two lovers in *Romeo and Juliet* and angered that a simple word could start a deadly feud. For *Macbeth,* students were incredulous that Macbeth would be so greedy and evil and enjoyed Lady Macbeth's treachery as well. They rewrote the ending of *Romeo and Juliet* and even had a wedding for the couple. For *Macbeth,* they set scenes in modern times. In all these circumstances, students made Shakespeare their own. The more they read and talked about the text, the more they realized they *could* read and talk about the text. In the beginning, true, it was slow going, but much of what they needed was simply to be encouraged and shown *how* to read Shakespeare's language: paraphrasing, summarizing, and clearing up misunderstandings with text.

Prior to beginning *Macbeth,* I organized a school-wide Shakespeare competition, where all my students were required to memorize and perform a soliloquy of between fifteen and twenty lines from one of Shakespeare's plays. I thought it another way for them to interact with Shakespeare and experience a competition that focused on their ability to speak well rather than their ability to play a sport.

Students had the time over winter break to memorize their monologues and then performed them in front of a panel at the Huntington Theatre in Boston (the school has a partnership with the renowned theatre). The partnership with the Huntington Theatre provided the unique opportunity for my students to write and produce their own theatrical showcase. Twice monthly, students would make the trip to the theatre to work with directors and actors. It was a school tradition that the sophomore class's production was a compilation of original work that was performed for the school community, including parents and other supporters, as one of the last events of the school year.

The eventual school winner, Antwan, advanced to the state semifinal Shakespeare competition, sponsored by the Boston English-Speaking Union, where he placed in the top ten. Antwan was the only student of color and one of only two from a Boston public school. Each performance he gave—he played Romeo who, upon finding Juliet dead, drinks poison and kills himself—was compelling and well acted. In addition to his monologue, he also memorized and delivered sonnet number 130: "My mistress' eyes are nothing like the sun."

While he did not win the final competition, Antwan experienced a transformation. As a student who always struggled with reading, Antwan focused on his monologue, even practicing it the night before the competition on the sidelines of a basketball game. Initially, he had been hesitant and did not want to participate, until he won the school-wide competition. His classmates cheered him on, offering words of encouragement and constructive criticism. Also, before this competition, Antwan had seen himself able to achieve recognition and accomplishment solely through athletics. With the Shakespeare competition, however, his identity became grounded in that of an actor who could act using Shakespeare's words.

AFRICAN AMERICAN HISTORY/STEPPING STORIES

During the sophomore year, I continued to be distressed by my students' lack of awareness about African American history and cultural and literary traditions. Because my school had such a flexible curriculum, I decided to create a project that would culminate in a final showcase at the Huntington Theatre. Students would spend four months researching history from the viewpoint of an African American assigned to them and then construct monologues in a production called *Stepping Stories*.

I assigned subjects from the civil rights movement, from the Harlem Renaissance, and others that were obscure but that I felt students *needed* to know. I chose the civil rights movement primarily because so many catalysts for change were young people about the same age as my sophomores. I also wanted to move beyond the stock figures of African American history, so Martin Luther King, Jr., Harriet Tubman, and Malcolm X were not in this project. Instead, the gamut ranged from Sojourner Truth and Benjamin Banneker to Nella Larsen and Carter G. Woodson, among others. I also combined experiences and skills I thought indispensable to academic scholarship, among them research, monologue writing, and performance.

The first trip we made to implement the project was to a neighborhood branch of the Boston Public Library. While some students had visited a library, few knew how to find a book, scan for evidence, take notes, or cite references. So we spent time familiarizing students with a library's layout and we met with a librarian who pointed out the location of young adult books. During subsequent classes, I focused minilessons around using indices to find information, determining if a book was useful for a topic, and other issues that emerged as the project progressed. For example, they created timelines: a chronological one for their person's life and a historical one that detailed the significant events happening in their person's world during his or her lifetime.

In class, we watched the PBS documentary series *Eyes on the Prize*. My students were rightfully outraged by the treatment endured by African Americans during the sixties. This outrage sparked in-depth class discussions as students drew parallels to their current situations and circumstances.

On the Fridays when we worked with the Huntington Theatre, students began to shape the monologues they were writing. Relying on their research, students selected pivotal moments that they thought shaped their characters. For Nonie, who portrayed Fannie Lou Hamer, the moment was speaking to a group of young people to convince them to vote. Speaking as Hamer, the student wrote, "I wasn't scared about dying or getting put into jail—because it seemed like people have tried to kill me my whole life."

Another student, John, writing as Medgar Evers, selected the moment when Evers lay dying in his driveway after being shot. "Freedom has never been free. . . . I love my wife and my children with all my heart. And I would die, die gladly, if that would make a better life for them. And to think one shot is all it took to kill freedom."

This project also solidified the spirit of collaboration that kept these students working so well with each other for two years. They listened to each other's monologues, provided feedback and editing, and even practiced with each other in the weeks leading up to the performance. They waited patiently for their time to work with Linda, listening attentively to her instruction.

What was also such a privilege to observe was the students' transformation *into* their historical personalities. It happened after a rehearsal where we talked through the order of the performance. The exact moment occurred while students watched an exchange between their two peers portraying Booker T. Washington and W. E. B. Du Bois. Students suddenly began reacting and talking as if they *were* their characters.

On the night of the performance, nearly all the students had a parent or relative in attendance. Their monologues were delivered with courage and pride, and the audience called out or responded to particularly moving lines; at times, it resembled a church service. The stage was stark, with a set of three steps from which characters spoke. The monologues were interspersed with music appropriate to the time period. One of the pivotal moments came when the young man portraying Stokely Carmichael ascended a ladder and issued a call to action to other characters while accompanied by the strains of Jimi Hendrix's rendition of the "Star Spangled Banner." His demands for "Black Power" were echoed by the audience as the cast then silently clasped hands and simulated a sit-in, legs crossed, heads bowed. The performance concluded with monologues based on the experiences of Linda Brown and Thurgood Marshall. Although speaking to a group of African American lawyers in his monologue, his message was a rallying call for many others, cast and audience included. "I'm old and the burden is on you to continue to fight for our people. Strive to make changes and never be frightened to defend what is just. I wasn't—you mustn't be either."

THE OUTSIDE WORLD, INDEPENDENCE, AND FEELING VALUED

I did other things that contributed to my ability to make tremendous academic demands of my students and to their ability to deliver quality work. I arranged for them to regularly attend lectures, poetry readings, theatre and dance performances, book talks, and bookstores in the city. These events were bookended by preparatory and post-event classroom-based academic activities. I wanted my students to fully embrace the intellectual and cultural life if the city.

I also did things to make students feel valued. We celebrated each student's birthday. And I regularly called students and their families. It was important for me to connect with parents about their students' academic achievements and potential. I set aside two hours each Sunday to make phone calls. This practice was so common that on the occasional Sunday when I did not call, students would ask on Monday me if I had been sick or if I had forgotten. While I always gave parents an update on how their students were progressing in my class, I also talked about upcoming events, observations I had made about students, what students could be doing more of, how much I believed in the students. Parents were almost always receptive, promptly returning my call if they were not there, following up with me on conversations, asking what they could do to help their children. For example, one grandmother asked if I could send home a list of transitions so she could work on helping her granddaughter add them to her writing. I loved these calls. It was the opportunity to integrate families into what I was attempting to do within the classroom with their children. I seldom had difficulties, other than scheduling, in engaging parents in conversations about their children.

CONCLUSIONS

For two years, I worked diligently to create an intentional community within my classroom, where academic excellence was the norm. This intentional community took its shape from efforts to keep students connected to their peer group, providing feedback in order to achieve high academic results, and my enduring belief in the capabilities of my students.

When I first began teaching, one of the few things I did know, even as a new teacher, was that my students could do challenging work. It was my job to show them how to do that work. Despite setbacks, my students came to regard themselves as academic achievers. They could articulate their pride in themselves as scholars, and performing well academically sometimes superseded performing well on the basketball court. Throughout the two years, I never lost my belief in my students. I felt that if I showed them how to be successful academically, if I gave them time and space to practice those skills and develop those tools, they would internalize those beliefs. I was able to integrate literature and history from the African American experience within my curriculum, allowing students every possible opportunity to realize the tremendous accomplishments and capabilities of people of color.

The community I created with my students can be replicated. Some suggestions for parents and community leaders wishing to extend and promote academic excellence include these:

1. Insist that students receive culturally grounded, quality education.

2. Dedicate a space for students and those wishing to work with them. This space must be welcoming, safe, and readily available at various times throughout the week to minimize the possibilities of scheduling difficulties. Also, populate that space with books students want to read, books that capture the lived experience of being a person of color in our world.

3. Support local talent: communities are full of budding writers and poets. Encourage them to make their work public through poetry slams, readings, and other avenues that promote the abilities of the community. Make the performances family-friendly: provide childcare so that all family members may attend.

4. Promote a culture of academic excellence: students, teenage Black men in particular, need to regularly see people reading, talking about reading, discussing high academic expectations, refusing to settle for mediocrity in the classroom. In these communities, being a successful student is expected, not an anomaly. Communities can have regular celebrations that recognize student achievement. A relentless pursuit of excellence must move beyond the classroom and into the community, where it will resonate consistently with students.

5. Find the people within the community willing to supplement classroom learning with their own expertise. Numerous people in the community are willing to help students with math, writing, life skills, etc. Communities must recognize their own strengths and then connect those experts with students. Some of those community experts

might also be relied upon to teach others to read, as the inability to read is a troubling obstacle.

6. Parents and communities must maintain an unflagging belief in the ability and potential of the children within the community. This belief will lead to the belief that children deserve culturally grounded, quality education. From there, parents and community leaders must be relentless in their desire to provide that education for their children.

The final assignment of their sophomore year was to write auto-biographies of themselves as readers and to conclude with a letter to me that evaluated our two years together. These letters were affirming and humbling, providing tangible proof of the power of an intentional community focused on academic achievement for students of color.

One student, Jerome, summed it up in the following manner: "I want you to know that there [has] not been a teacher that has pushed me to WRITE so much. Now thanks to you I did good on the MCAS and I still feel great about myself."

In his letter to me, Max wrote:

> Over these two [years] we have learned so much that it seems like you've been with me for ten years. . . . Speaking of curriculum, you always seem to make the right decision for things we need to study. . . . You always pushed us to do our best. From stacking us up with essays to practice for the MCAS or giving us Open Response to practice more for the MCAS. . . . I am extremely happy that we were original and did something about our people. . . . I also enjoyed how you taught history from the Black point of view. I'm glad we didn't learn it out of textbooks but instead you did research, which shows that you were learning too. . . . To me personally you were like a mentor because you were the one who always suggested books for me to read. Plus you opened me up to poetry.

Another student, Tahara, wrote

> Before I came to this school I read books but I only read them because I had to. But now I read books because they are interesting to me.

Finally, John had this to say:

> Thank you for not being afraid to be straight up with us. Telling us exactly how it is and will be. Thanks for the 5 minute brakes [sic], snack time, Lit. circle, "Tears of a Tiger," "The Outsiders." Thanks for being you. Thanks for giving me your number to call whenever I needed, thanks for being there when I needed, Thanks for telling me and making me believe that I am a good, and will be great writer.

These letters and this account are proof that, even in this age of high-stakes testing and increased accountability, students, particularly these students of African American and Caribbean American descent, can become intellectuals, produce high-quality work, learn about their people, and achieve on high-stakes tests. They only need to be shown how.

NOTES

1. Theresa Perry, Claude Steele, and Asa Hilliard III, *Young, Gifted and Black: Promoting High Achievement Among African-American Students* (Boston: Beacon, 2003), 93.
2. Ibid., 107.
3. Ibid., 95.
4. See lesson plan at http://www.readwritethink.org/lessons/lesson_view .asp?id=1041.

WORKS CITED

Beals, Melba Patillo. 1994. *Warriors don't cry.* New York: Simon & Schuster.

Beers, Kylene. 2003. *When kids can't read, what teachers can do: A guide for teachers 6–12.* Portsmouth, NH: Heinemann.

Daniels, Harvey. 2002. *Literature circles: Voice and choice in book clubs and reading groups.* Ontario, Canada: Stenhouse.

Draper, Sharon. 2002. *Darkness before dawn.* New York: Simon & Schuster.

———. 1998. *Forged by fire.* New York: Simon & Schuster.

———. 1996. *Tears of a tiger.* New York: Simon & Schuster.

Frey, Darcy. 1994. *The last shot: City streets, basketball dreams.* New York: Houghton Mifflin.

Gaines, Ernest. 1994. *A lesson before dying.* New York: Vintage.

Harvey, Stephanie, and Anne Goudvis. 2003. *Strategies that work: Teaching comprehension to enhance understanding.* Ontario, Canada: Stenhouse.

Kidd, Sue Monk. 2003. *The secret life of bees.* New York: Penguin.

Lee, Harper. 2006 (1960). *To kill a mockingbird.* New York: HarperCollins.

Perry, Theresa, Claude Steele, and Asa Hilliard III. 2003. *Young, gifted, and Black: Promoting high achievement among African-American students.* Boston: Beacon Press.

Twain, Mark. 2004 (1876). *The adventures of Tom Sawyer.* New York: Barnes & Noble.

Williams, Juan. 2004. *Eyes on the prize: America's civil rights years, 1954–1965.* New York: Penguin.

7

Is This School?[1]

Alicia Carroll

As an African American woman teaching in an urban school system for the past nine years, I'm committed to the education and achievement of all children. I'm especially committed to providing engaging, challenging, inquiry-based learning experiences for urban children who are the most vulnerable and at the most risk of being left behind. It is these children who enter my classroom as bright, intelligent, articulate, inquisitive learners, and I am working to provide an environment where I can continue to foster all of these qualities and that love of learning that they already bring with them.

I'm going to talk about three things: first, recognizing and building on cultural capital in the classroom; second, setting up the classroom environment; finally, creating three curriculum units that illustrate what I'm talking about.

CULTURAL CAPITAL

What is *cultural capital?* The term comes from Pierre Bourdieu, a French sociologist who introduced the idea of cultural capital in 1973. According to Bourdieu, cultural capital is simply the knowledge, skills, education, high expectations, or any advantages that give a person a higher status in society.

But what might be capital in my culture may not get me anywhere in your culture, and vice versa. So, to me, *cultural capital* also means everything that encompasses who you are. Whether or not that capital is valued when you walk into a given environment can potentially determine your success or failure. This point is illustrated for me by this little quotation here—"School is all wrong—they ask you what you don't know, not what you know. When I took the test in sixth grade, they asked, "Where is Cape Fear?" I said I didn't know but that I could give the names of the twelve apostles, and I did." Likewise, when any child walks into a school or a classroom, we seldom take the time to find out what they do know.

MY CULTURAL CAPITAL

In my case, my cultural capital first came from my family and their southern roots. I come from a family of educators: aunts, uncles, and cousins who grew up and were educated in the segregated South. When you walked into a school building in the South and your teachers were also African American, they understood and valued your cultural capital because it was theirs. They were invested in your success and created an environment that ensured that success. This meant that teachers would imbue you with the belief that it was primary that you get an education, and that you had to work hard to make it happen.

Although I grew up in Cambridge, Massachusetts, this understanding was instilled in me through the language that people used all the time. My great-grandfather, Columbus Hall Crooms, was the mayor of Eatonville, Florida, one of the oldest Black towns in the United States, and was at one point given an honorary degree by Yale University. I will never forget what he always used to say: "You have to work twice as hard to be considered half as good," and "Without an education your opportunities in this lifetime will be limited." It was always emphasized and understood in my family that you would graduate from college and then come back and work in your community. Like the phrase posted above the chapel door of many Black colleges, you were to "enter to learn, depart to serve."

What I learned from my family was that Black teachers in the South valued what you brought from home, but they also knew that they had to enlarge your cultural capital in order for you to be successful in the dominant culture, outside the security of a familiar environment. For my family, this meant exposing me and my brothers to all kinds of experiences—from museums and symphonies and plays to living overseas in Iran for four years and traveling throughout the Middle East and parts of Europe. My cultural capital began with a knowledge and pride in who I am and was enlarged through many experiences for me to have a knowledge and pride of who I am in the larger world. It is this that inspires me and informs my teaching.

CHILDREN'S CULTURAL CAPITAL

Who provides children with cultural capital, the attitudes and knowledge that make the educational system a *comfortable, familiar* place in which they can succeed easily?

Are we valuing the cultural capital that kids are already coming in with? Or, are we even recognizing it? I've heard some teachers say, "Oh, that kid doesn't know this." "They're supposed to come in knowing their letters/numbers/colors." They're already looking at the kids from a deficit model, what the kids don't know as opposed to what they do know—asking about Cape Fear and getting a list of the twelve apostles, and then wondering what's wrong with the child and whether they might need an Individual Education Plan.

What's important is to figure out how to connect with families. This can happen in different ways at different ages and grade levels.

At the kindergarten/first-grade level, many teachers go on home visits before school begins in September, and this is particularly important at this age, because it is the child's first introduction to school, and if the student is an only or oldest child, it is the introduction to the school for his or her family as well. I've been fortunate to be able to do this and to be able to spend time talking with the child as well as his or her family. I find out what that child is interested in. The very first question I ask at the home visit is, "If you could learn about anything in the world, what would that be?" Then I ask the parents about their child: "Tell me about Amir. He's already told me about himself. Is there anything else you'd like to say?" I try to listen to their stories and acknowledge that they are their child's first teacher. This way, we can connect and build a relationship that will support their child's academic learning. And, so far, I've never met a family that didn't want their child to achieve.

The home visit, or experience of finding out what the child is interested in, pays dividends from the very start. I'll share the example of one of my very first students at the Mission Hill School, because this one sticks in my mind. When Amir told me he loved spiders and ants and snails and going outside to learn about living things, he gave me a lot of information about how to begin to engage him. Right away, I had the information about Amir's cultural capital, that is, what he knows and likes to learn about when it's up him. I could begin to think about embedding those things into the classroom environment and into the curriculum during the school year in ways that would take his existing cultural capital, enlarge it, and connect it with school. Actually, what I did was go out and buy a turtle. He was a big pond slider, perfect for a kindergarten classroom. I also got books about turtles in the classroom. The moment Amir came to the door on his first day of school, he looked through the doorway and saw the turtle in its habitat in the glass fish tank, with the word "turtle" on it. He looked back at his family and said, "Is this *school?*" Then he told his family, "Okay, good-bye, you can leave now!" and left them at the door. The turtle helped make the classroom a comfortable, familiar place where Amir wanted to be because it was already part of who he is and what he brings. The classroom was a place that had things he was interested in learning about and became a place where he felt he could take risks in his learning and could deepen his knowledge.

Getting to know the families is critical. It helps me figure out ways in which I can include them—in the classroom and the curriculum. This is where parents begin to learn *with* their kids. It happens throughout the curriculum, but it begins here. Their voices are being heard; they know that I'm hearing them, that I'm listening to them, and that I'm listening to their child. This is another building block of cultural capital.

I send home a weekly newsletter describing what we've learned in the classroom. Every Friday we have a group meeting, and I ask the children, "What would you want your parents and other people who are reading the newsletter to know about your learning?" The kids share while I take write down exactly what they say, and that goes in a section of the newsletter. For all the times I've done this, I continue to be amazed at the brilliant things they say and at the way their minds work. When I listen to the kids talk about their learning, I feel like *I* learn more each time about the *power of their ideas* (to quote the title of a book by Deborah Meier[2]).

Here are some parent responses to the newsletter:

I get real satisfaction from seeing how excited he is about what
is he learning and doing at school. It is a wonderful thing he
can share with me when he comes home. He is very thoughtful and analytical in the way he talks about it.

—*Devin's mom*

One day Emily and I were looking at a picture book about a
dancer. She remembered seeing the little dancer sculpture by
Degas, and imitated the pose of the dancer in the sculpture.

—*Emily's mom*

This is an important connection back to home. Parents often say
to me, "Alicia, I love getting the newsletter on Mondays. I always go
straight to the section where the children talk about what they're
learning. I feel like I'm learning along with my child. You can hear the
voices of the kids coming right out of the paper." One parent told me,
"I have learned more about Egypt from my child than I ever dreamed
I'd know. My child explained to me the difference between the upper
and lower Nile and the architectural difference between the Nubian
and Egyptian pyramids!"

This, instead of the deficit model, is the *asset* model—the cultural
capital at home becomes a valuable part of classroom culture, and the
cultural capital learned in the classroom goes home: what the child
knows and loves, plus what the parents know and do, enriches the
curriculum. The asset model equation says "your way + my way =
more."

SETTING THE CLASSROOM ENVIRONMENT

The minute you walk through the doors of a classroom, there's a message being conveyed, and it is conveyed through what the kids are doing, what's on the walls, and the quality of interactions going on.

This is a print-rich environment, where four-, five- and six-year-
olds have first experiences with the connection between objects, activities, and written words. I try to set up my classroom each year so
that children are at the center of the learning that is going on. The
physical space needs to be clean, welcoming, and aesthetically pleas-
ing, full of sensory experiences. Parents come in and say, "Put me to

work." They help paint walls, sand and paint furniture, put up coat hooks, set up the classroom library, label shelves. Through this process, parents feel a sense of belonging, that they are part of the classroom and not just a visitor who has to check in at the office.

Children are involved in setting up the classroom community from the beginning and setting up the norms for the way that community will function. The classroom functions in a democratic fashion, and students learn how to take charge of their own learning. They learn to self-regulate their behavior.

What is going on in the classroom that tells parents and visitors that kids are engaged in their learning? Is it reflected on the walls of the classroom? Is the work high quality? Are the kids excited about learning? Are they proud? Do they want to talk about their work?

One of my fundamental beliefs about curriculum is that it should be a vehicle to expose students to many different experiences. I have intentionally created a classroom that is a *comfortable, familiar* place where students have many different learning entry points (whether that point is a spider, or a special book, or pictures of themselves), so that they are soon ready to take more risks and are eager to engage in learning about things unfamiliar to them. I've met them where they are, and now we're ready to experience and learn about their community and the larger world.

Parents are not always clear about what their children are learning in school, about whether their children's overall education is engaging and challenging, sub-standard and boring, or meeting grade-level expectations with benchmarks along the way. Good early childhood classrooms (Pre-K through first grade) are developmentally appropriate. Developmentally appropriate classrooms are characterized by the following:

- Children's interests are at the center of all learning.
- Children's ideas and work are taken seriously.
- Children share their ideas and are given opportunities to bring those ideas to fruition.
- Children create the norms of the classroom.
- Children work cooperatively and independently.
- Cultural differences (racial and linguistic) are celebrated.
- Teachers provide an environment where children feel comfortable and safe enough to take risks in their learning.

- Children are encouraged to speak, participate, and share their knowledge with each other.
- Teachers do less talking and more listening: students should do more talking than the teacher!
- Learning from mistakes is valued and seen as an opportunity to deepen children's knowledge.
- Children are exposed to a local and global education: they start with themselves and connect to the international community.
- Exploration, discovery, inquiry, and investigation are valued by all.
- The classroom is inviting and colorful, with a variety of learning opportunities.
- The classroom reflects all forms of communication: reading, writing, speaking, listening to each other, and presenting work.
- Knowledge is connected throughout the learning experiences.
- Teacher and students learn together.
- Teachers model their learning for students: students see that learning is a lifelong endeavor.
- Children publish their own stories.
- Evidence of science, math, and language arts is visible in the learning environment.
- Vocabulary should be posted on word walls in conjunction with theme-related activities.
- Opportunities for art, music, dance, drama, woodworking, and other sensory activities are visible.
- Parents are welcome and encouraged to be learners as well as participants in their child's learning.
- The curriculum connects to children's lives and their everyday experiences.
- Kids have plenty of opportunities to practice, use, and demonstrate mastery of basic skills.

THE CURRICULUM

In order to cover all the material we're being asked to teach kids, I think we have to be interdisciplinary in our approach to teaching. For example, a study of structures becomes the vehicle for teaching reading, writing, mathematics, science, social studies, art, and music. This approach allows me to make sure that

- Children are at the *center* of the learning.
- There are multiple entry points.
- I can make adaptations and modifications for all learners.
- We're meeting the standards for state and local frameworks.
- The curricula engage kids at a deeper level.
- Kids become experts.
- The data show that kids are demonstrating academic progress.

As a teacher teaching this way, I know that

- I need to research and understand the focus topic deeply and on multiple levels.
- I have to translate these big ideas into a language that four- and five-year-olds can understand—making the invisible visible.
- The ongoing assessments inform my teaching.
- What I know, in terms of both content and pedagogical knowledge, is embedded in my teaching.
- It's important for me to collaborate with colleagues and specialists who are working with the same children.

Every school has a framework in place. At Young Achievers (YA) Science and Math School, there are three school-based curricula in place: Young Naturalists, Water, and Structures. Additionally, in January, there is an assembly in honor of Martin Luther King Jr., at which each class makes a presentation on a social justice theme.

Out of these three units emerged the following three curriculum units. I'm going to describe them a little bit and also describe how I made some of the connections between my ideas, the children's interests, and the frameworks of the existing curricula.

LEARNING TO READ NATURE'S BOOK

The first project I'll describe is a curriculum I took from the YA framework and developed with my colleague Bisse Bowman. We called it

"Learning to Read Nature's Book." The curriculum integrates sculpture, the natural world, and social justice.

A Teacher's Thinking Process

I had become extremely interested in the work of a local sculptor, Fern Cunningham. She is the creator of the "Step on Board" sculpture of Harriet Tubman in the South End neighborhood of Boston. I became very interested in her as an artist, and I spent a summer in her studio, taking pictures, talking to her about her work and her inspiration. And I was so excited about her that I knew I wanted to teach kids about sculpture. But I also knew that in the fall at Young Achievers the focus would be on the Young Naturalists curriculum. I spent a great deal of time trying to figure out how I was going to teach sculpture, which I felt very passionate about, and just couldn't conceptualize what the young naturalists curriculum would look like.

Then, one day, I received a mailing from the Forest Hills Cemetery about their sculpture path, with pictures of sculptures made out of natural materials. So I went on one of their walking tours, and the "aha" moment came—I began to see how I could connect my passion with the requirements. Before I left the tour of the sculpture path, I met Cecily Miller, the director of education at the cemetery, and we began to set up a partnership. Soon thereafter, my colleague, Bisse Bowman (the art teacher at YA) showed me a book by Andy Goldsworthy, who creates sculptures from natural materials, and that was the beginning of "Learning to Read Nature's Book."

I started brainstorming ideas for integrating nature and sculpture and began to draw a preliminary curriculum web to help me visualize how my ideas would encompass the frameworks. Shortly before school began that fall, I approached Bisse about collaborating on this curriculum, and we began planning together. Later on we were able to share our ideas with the rest of the kindergarten team. The full story of this was published in the winter 2006 issue of *Community Works Journal.*[2]

We focused on three sculptors whose work encompassed the themes of social and environmental justice and whose cultures connected to kids in the classroom: Fern Cunningham, Andy Goldsworthy, and Maya Lin, the Chinese American artist who designed the Vietnam Memorial in Washington, D.C., and the Civil Rights Monument in Montgomery, Alabama.

The point I want to make here is that it is possible for teachers to integrate what they are passionate about into existing frameworks. Throughout the three months of exploration within this curriculum, I still had to teach math, literacy, science, and readers and writers workshops. I was still following the children's interests with the frameworks in mind, and making sure the kids were meeting all the benchmarks along the way. As exciting as the curriculum was, the kids still had to acquire their basic skills. As an African American educator teaching in an urban school, I feel a deep responsibility to make sure that our children have a strong foundation of skills and higher-level thinking they will need as they move on through elementary school.

Some Highlights of the Curriculum

Children made weekly visits to the study site at Forest Hills Cemetery to study the flora and the fauna and the sculptures created with natural materials.

Literacy

- Students recorded their observations in their science notebooks through dictation, drawing, and sounding out and writing words (Writers' Workshop).
- They wrote in their journals, created interactive writing charts, brainstormed words, and painted pictures to create a classroom alphabet.
- Children developed literacy skills, phonemic awareness (letters, sounds, and writing skills) in the context of what they were learning.
- They read big books, fiction and nonfiction, rookie-reader science books, poems, charts, and songs that developed their comprehension skills (part of Readers' Workshop).

Science

- Children developed the skills of inquiry and science vocabulary (*pudding stone, hemlock cones, path, rustle, exo-skeleton, emerge, life-cycle, habitat*).
- Children drew maps of Forest Hills and served as guides for their parents there (social studies, mapping skills, language skills).

Math

We followed the BPS Investigations Math units (TERC). The children's collections of chestnuts, pine cones, hemlock cones, acorns, chestnut burrs, and stones were easily incorporated into the math units (sorting, patterns, geometry, number sense, counting, graphing).

- Children continued developing their math language (*shape, patterns, graphs, 2- and 3-D models, repeat, predict, sort,* and names of shapes).

THE MTEPE (BOAT) PROJECT

Our second big project was the *Mtepe* project (*Mtepe* is the Swahili word for "boat"). This was an outgrowth a larger project begun three years ago by my colleague and friend Lucy Montgomery, also a social studies and history teacher in Boston. We researched the historical connections between Africa and China through the trade routes. Three years ago, we spent three weeks traveling the Silk Road in China, from Beijing to Xian to Kashgar, with a group of teachers through Primary Source in nearby Watertown. In the summer of 2004, we traveled to the East African coast, thanks to funding from the Fulbright Foundation through Boston University and a Boston Fund for Teachers grant.

We set out to discover the connections between Africa and China, with a desire to highlight Africa's participation in silk route trade, via land and ocean. This goes back to teachers' passion: our "aha moment" came in China when we decided to distill our research into a children's book we're calling *Malindi's Journey,* about a giraffe who traveled from the East African coast to China in the fifteenth century. This journey is documented in Chinese historical records, and our research so far, in libraries and oral histories, has indicated that the giraffe most likely made this voyage across the Indian Ocean on an *mtepe,* an ocean-going trade vessel. We have begun to develop curriculum about Africa, China, Islam, and the Silk Road. The boat project below is one example of this curriculum.

I had just returned from East Africa about two weeks before school started in 2004, and all I could think of was that I wanted to build a boat with the kids in my classroom. When I discovered that John Rowse, another of my colleagues at Young Achievers was also a boat builder, I knew I had a vehicle (so to speak) for our water curriculum, and would also be a perfect connection to the structures unit later that year. John was also interested in teaching his fourth- and fifth-graders math and science skills through boat building. I talked John, and we decided to build a boat.

Highlights of This Curriculum

- Integration of boats with the water curriculum (a natural fit)
- Opportunities for students to practice their math, science, and visual perception skills
- Explicit global and cultural connections (Africa, China, Islam)
- Journal writing and student reflection on their work (writing and literacy)
- A special *Mtepe* log for the kindergarteners to record all kinds of things: observational drawing, labeling the parts, drawing and labeling the tools, observing, drawing and naming shapes and materials
- Cross-age learning experiences between younger and older kids
- Parental involvement (parents helped with the building)

After reading *The Alphabet of Boats,* a Readers' Workshop book, children worked in cooperative groups to experiment with building different types of boats in the block area.

STRUCTURES

Again, I used the existing framework and enlarged the learning. We studied local structures and architecture in our community (our school, the mosque in Roxbury) and structures of the world. For example, a Mayan temple, Egyptian pyramids, the Leaning Tower of Pisa, mosques in East Africa and China, the Great Wall of China, and the Greek Parthenon. We read big books, both fiction and nonfiction, and watched videos about these famous structures. We located the structures on a map and a globe, identifying countries and cities. Children then worked in cooperative groups, and each got to choose a structure to learn more about and build.

Children started by building, and their questions emerged:

- How strong can I make a structure?
- How many blocks can I pile on top of a structure before it falls down?
- Can I build a structure large enough for my body to fit in?
- How long can I make it?

Through all these activities, children continued to develop their academic and inquiry skills and their content knowledge. Along the way, I continued to assess the students' learning, so that I could make modifications when necessary, provide direct teaching, and ensure that the students were meeting the benchmarks. This is critical to understand. One of the misunderstandings of progressive, project-based learning is that direct instruction and basic skills fall by the wayside. I'm saying that project-based education can be engaging and inspiring at the same time as teachers teach kids to master basic skills.

ASSESSMENT

Assessment is used as a tool to inform instruction for teachers. It allows a teacher to know where students are in their learning process and what the next steps are for instruction. To assess all of the learning, we used portfolios, student and parent interviews, and Boston Public School assessments, including Concepts about Print, Developmental Reading Assessment, Writing Sample, and Boston citywide math and science assessments.

What the data showed was that students were all at grade level or above level, according to the assessments, and that there was a significant improvement over the previous school year. Worth mentioning is that their reading comprehension skills and vocabulary were notably high.

TEACHERS AND STUDENTS AS INTELLECTUALS

As teachers we must remember that we are never finished as students. Teachers must also think of themselves as scholars. In order to develop more meaningful, intellectually rigorous and engaging curricula, we must research information and have the opportunity to think deeply about the content. Although we often have neither the time nor the access to resources to conduct our own research, we have to find ways to connect what we're passionate about with what we're being asked to teach students. I believe this is how we'll awaken our students' passion for learning.

Teachers need to translate the standards and frameworks from paper to actual change in classroom practices. Engaging kids at a deeper level allows them to see themselves as intellectuals and understand that learning is a lifelong process. The great Brazilian educator Paulo Freire spoke of reading the world as well as the word. We should look at our students not as mere recipients of knowledge handed down from above, but as people capable of constructing meaning and producing knowledge.

We want to broaden our students' scope of the world—whoever our students are. Our students—Black, Asian, Latino, White—should have the right and freedom to know the world, beginning with themselves. When this is so, they will be able to step into the shoes of others and begin to construct knowledge that is authentic and thereby a new reality. This is the real standard we should meet.

NOTES

1. To see this article with wonderful pictures that capture the quality of the children's work, go to www.achievementseminars.com/seminar_series _2005_2006/download.htm.
2. Deborah Meier, *The Power of Their Ideas: Lessons for America from a Small School in Harlem* (Boston: Beacon Press, 2002).

8

Stories of Collaboration and Research within an Algebra Project Context

Offering Quality Education to Students Pushed to the Bottom of Academic Achievement

Joan T. Wynne and Janice Giles

In an interview in 1981, former SNCC field secretary Charlie Cobb Jr. reminisced about the lessons young African Americans learned in the sixties:

> What we had learned essentially was that the things that affected blacks in Ruleville, Greenwood, or Sharkey County, Mississippi, didn't just stop at the county line or the state line. What we really had was a national structure. The sheriff and the Ku Klux Klan and White Citizens Council were all tied into the Congress and the president, and even if we got everybody registered to vote in Sunflower County it wasn't going to provide the complete answer for black people. We were beginning to see the relationship between economics and politics.[1]

As we have built partnerships across university and public school boundaries to create models of quality education for the disenfranchised, like Cobb, we have been reminded of the roots and the multiple layers of politics, power, and privilege that trap our youngsters into cycles of unequal and inferior education. Those structural forces at work in Mississippi and the nation in the sixties and in centuries before still plague urban and rural schools in the twenty-first century. This chapter attempts to tell the story of the challenges and triumphs of working within such a context to create and demand quality education for the progeny of slaves and sharecroppers as well as for other children denied academic excellence.

My early educational background was in literature. So I believe in the power of story. A character from Barry Lopez's *Crow and Weasel* says, "Sometimes people need stories more than food to stay alive."[2] I'm one of those people. Story keeps me intellectually and spiritually alive. And for me, research is a story. Some researchers tell that story in numbers—some tell it in narrative. Some believe numbers are sacred; some believe narrative is; and still others believe nothing is. Regardless of the form, though, the research story comes from a human who goes into and out of his or her project with biases. For all researchers come to those studies with specific cultural experiences, presuppositions, and delusions.

My experience of growing up in a segregated South influenced my personal and professional life. It was a south of "White only" water fountains, restrooms, and public spaces; a place of White supremacy; of Blacks in the back of the bus; a place of public lynchings and secret murders; a place of governmental doublespeak; of public universities refusing to admit Blacks into their institutions; a place where six-year-olds had to be escorted by the National Guard to walk safely through the doors of public schools. All of these factors from my lived experience helped shape my sense of what needs to be researched—and what cultural assumptions undergird a research and educational agenda—and ultimately helped lead me to the present research project.

That particular shaping also has persuaded me that ethical research is more than just an abstract theory. Although it too often gets cloaked in esoteric discourse, research is formed within a specific context of socio-political experiences and realities.

The poet Rumi says, "We have all walked in different gardens and knelt at different graves."[3] Those individual experiences of gardens and graves largely shape who we are—not only as humans but also as researchers—and help determine what it is we choose to investigate, what it is we're hoping to find, and what the biases are that we bring to the table of research.

In her 1999 book, *Decolonizing Methodologies: Research & Indigenous People*, researcher Linda Smith indicates that as a Maori woman from New Zealand, her personal story of resisting and transforming methods of oppression has shaped her research. She suggests that sometimes when we frame research within a specific scientific or disciplinary approach, we forget that all of it, for urban and indigenous people across the globe, is deeply embedded in complex and multiple layers of imperial and colonial practices.[4]

Unconscious colonial attitudes are often reflected in research journals that feature too many studies which seem stuck on discovering the deficits or dysfunctions of families of color, living in poverty. This propensity has created a sense in indigenous communities that research is a dirty word.[5]

UNIVERSITY PARTNERSHIP
WITH THE ALGEBRA PROJECT

In the spirit of countering that practice of "dirty research," the Center for Urban Education and Innovation at Florida International University (FIU), through a research grant awarded by the Urban Educators Corps, chose to investigate the work of Dr. Bob Moses and his Algebra Project (AP) in a ninth-grade classroom in one of the nation's largest metropolitan school systems. The system operates in a state that holds the record for the second-highest number of high school dropouts in the nation.[6] FIU is a large public university whose student population is majority Latino/Latina. The extended collaboration is an attempt to create a school-based, university-affiliated school reform, in which the accountability of the reform rests upon producing high academic achievement for students through four years of high school with "students standing on their own two feet" in college.[7] In this reform, the university comes to the school house. Professors, researchers, center partners work in the classroom with the students, alongside the high school teacher. Theories, curricula, and pedagogy are worked out inside the classroom with students. In this model, the university leaves its ivory tower and becomes intimately involved with its real constituents, testing knowledge, shaping and re-shaping its visions of reality to consciously contribute to the public good.

THE CENTER AND THE ALGEBRA PROJECT

For decades, a multitude of educators, governments, foundations, and school systems have been concerned about creating more effective learning environments for disenfranchised students. But as Charles Payne discovered during his five-year study of the massive Chicago School Reform Effort, there has been "so much reform, so little change."[8] Our experiences and research in urban schools suggest the same conclusion.[9] That is, until we investigated the work of Bob Moses and the Algebra Project. In fact, Payne cites AP as one of the few successful projects involved in Chicago's huge reform effort.[10]

AP is steeped in experiential learning pedagogy that, since Dewey, has proven effective in most disciplines. Within that context Moses and AP have developed imaginative approaches, responsive to youth culture, to teach mathematics to students who have been tracked out of higher-level abstract thinking. Moses and AP are doing what very few others dare—demanding excellence from children at the bottom instead of settling for their meeting minimum standards. But what is radical about AP's approach is its philosophy that the only ones who can really demand the kind of education they need and the kind of changes needed to get it are the students, their parents, and their community.[11] Moses believes that the young people must create a culture in which they begin to make a demand on themselves and then on the larger society and so create a kind of "earned insurgency."[12]

That philosophy puts the power in the hands of the people who are being abused by inadequate education, not in the hands of well-meaning advocates, or worse, in the hands of people who are intent on maintaining a "sharecropper" education for the descendents of slaves or other children of color.[13] The center believes that few in reform efforts fully comprehend this crucial component. Student and parent voices typically are either not invited or rarely taken seriously in the decision-making process in school reform. Though many districts are establishing parent academies, there often is distrust in the capacity of the disenfranchised to create powerful learning communities. And where there might be trust, there is little experience in organizing communities to address quality education for its children. The Algebra Project has been founded upon a long tradition of grass-roots organizing and has developed, as an integral part of its program, strategies for organizing parents and students to demand academic excellence.

Central to AP is the belief that "a real breakthrough would not make us happy if it did not deeply and seriously empower the target population to demand access to literacy for everyone. That is what is driving the project."[14] Many of us do not understand the profundity of that belief. Too often in school reform we are caught up in believing that improving instruction, empowering teachers, developing school leadership, encouraging teachers and administrators to share decision making, and other facets of educational change will transform low-performing schools. Certainly these components are significant in whole-school change, but they are not sufficient. When community and student demand for excellence for everyone is not organized and sustained, the other strategies for change provide only fleeting results, if any, for disenfranchised children.

In her five-year study of two school reform efforts in South Carolina, Pauline Lipman observed numerous progressive reform components operating within the two schools. However, at the end of the five years, she found that the academic achievement of African American students actually decreased during that time. She indicated that the failure to address the absence of community power and privilege within the schools played a significant role in thwarting the other reform components.[15] AP works within this essential dimension of school reform. Its work is a deliberate attempt to prove to the nation that all children, no matter how poor or how alienated from the society at large, can and will learn higher-level mathematics, given the appropriate curriculum, pedagogy, and support. A present example of AP's success is found at Mississippi's Lanier High School where large numbers of students take trigonometry and introductory engineering.[16] Eighty-five percent of AP's 2006 cohort graduates from Lanier successfully completed their first year of college.[17] In essence, AP is changing the story about America's disenfranchised children and communities.

EARLIER RESEARCH STUDIES OF AP

In a five-year study funded by the National Science Foundation (NSF), researchers found that AP students in several large cities around the country performed at a higher level when compared to the general population. The AP students enroll in ninth- and tenth-grade mathematics courses at a significantly higher rate. They enroll in college preparatory courses at twice the rate, and they pass state mathematics exams at significantly higher rates. The researchers also found that teachers who were taught the AP pedagogy and curriculum became more effective in the classrooms with higher levels of mathematical conceptual understanding by students.[18]

THE LOCAL CHALLENGE

The size of the local school system and its history of failing schools within poor neighborhoods (thirty-nine chronically low-performing schools) make this system an excellent model for addressing the issues that face urban schools across the country. A majority of the system's students are ethnic minorities; a high percentage of them are poor; many are from immigrant backgrounds; and 62 percent speak English as their second language.[19]

STRUGGLES IN FORMING THE COLLABORATION

Although the system's superintendent proclaimed at the first district level partners' meeting, "Bob Moses, you are a gift to this county," it took subsequent months of meetings with other district and school administrators, students, and parents for Moses to finally begin his AP work at Eagle High School. Eagle is located in a neighborhood where some of the students are African American and some are Latino, but many more of its students are bilingual Haitians whose first language is Kreyol. Moses and his FIU teaching fellow, Mario Eraso, began the process of bringing AP to Eagle High School in September 2006 in a classroom with twenty-four students who were achieving at the bottom quartile of academic measures (state tests and grade averages). The only criterion for selecting the members of the cohort was that they be in the bottom quartile.

PARENT VISITS

A significant piece of the partnership has been meeting with parents to explain the program and the kind of commitment that it takes from parents and students for success in mathematics. These meetings are crucial in building the demand side of the quest for academic excellence. In the beginning, however, meeting with cohort parents posed quite a challenge. Because student records and addresses are confidential, the school administration offered to contact parents to invite them to a dinner in August 2006, at which Dr. Moses could explain his program before the students started the school year. Over fifty parents were invited. One parent came. After that trial, a concerted effort was made to obtain phone numbers and addresses of students so that we could make home visits. It took months to go up and down the chain of command to obtain addresses and many visits to erroneous addresses, even to houses that did not exist, before finally getting correct addresses from the students themselves as Eraso and Moses tutored them in small groups. By the end of October 2006, twenty of the original twenty-four students' homes had been visited. These visits continued throughout the school year.

But finding the students' parents was just the tip of the iceberg of troubles confronted when attempting to unfold the project in the new location. Eagle's administration decided that the students needed to use the first six and one-half months of their ninth-grade mathematics class to prepare for the state's high-stakes test, the Florida Comprehensive Assessment Test (FCAT). Therefore, Moses and Eraso were allowed to work only as aides in the teacher-of-record's classroom to help the students prepare for the FCAT. The full AP curriculum and pedagogy finally began on March 19, 2007.

Visits to the cohort classroom in January, February, and the first part of March 2007, along with the visits to the class after March 19, yielded the following observations: Before instituting the curricular process of the Algebra Project with the cohort in March, a traditional pedagogy was used by the teacher-on-record. Students sat passively as the teacher advanced to new topics without pausing to check for student understanding. Just a few students participated. Those who did reproduced procedural mathematics but could not explain the meaning of their work. The students were intimidated by a teacher who repeatedly yelled at them to control the class. On the first week of the transition to AP in March, two different students asked Moses's assistant: "Why does Dr. Moses talk so softly?"[20]

The Algebra Project's curricular process is based on a shared student experience; therefore, in March, these ninth-graders used a bus fieldtrip to FIU as their first AP collective experience. It allowed students an opportunity to discuss among themselves the mathematics of the location of different landmarks found on the bus route taken the day of the fieldtrip. Students took careful notes that described the shared experience, simulating the detailed process a scientist or artist goes through to describe a phenomenon.

Once back in the classroom, the students drew iconic representations of the shared experience before being exposed to the symbolic representation of mathematics. Most of the work done by the instructors is to get students to think abstractly and to apply what they learn. The mechanism for this strategy, "people talk," involves students using their own informal language to describe what they observe. Following this stage, the teacher introduces "feature talk," technical mathematical language that allows students to communicate explicitly. Prior to the talk, however, the students produced a class trip line that graphically and pictorially illustrated the fieldtrip from their high school to the university. Colorful poster boards full of pictures serve as the context to learn the mathematics of integers. Mathematical objects, actions, and relationships are introduced.

For example, movement, an object, and moving, an action, are distinguished as students use displacement vectors, location integers, and addition. Mathematical relationships are developed, too, finally arriving at abstract formulations such as these, provided by Eraso:

- x_1 + delta x = x_2, where x_1 and x_2 are location integers assigned to landmarks on the trip line,
- delta x is the movement (left or right) needed to go from x_1 to x_2,
- and the symbols "+" and "=" mean "to move" and "to arrive," respectively[21]

Moses created the trip-line strategy while teaching in Boston in the 1980s. Later, with his team of mathematicians, he developed a consistent pedagogy that is explained in *Radical Equations* as the "Five Crucial Steps in the Algebra Project Curriculum Process."[22]

1. Physical Events: A trip taken by the students and teacher is the central experience of the transition curriculum designed to illustrate the concept to be learned.

2. Pictorial Representation/Modeling: Students move through a series of linked and increasingly abstract representations of the physical event, describing the event through pictures and everyday talk, which the teacher builds on to introduce the language of the discipline and symbolic representation.

3. Intuitive Language/"People Talk": Students are asked to discuss and write about the physical event in their own language.

4. Structured Language/"Feature Talk": This is "regimented" language aimed at explicitly selecting and encoding features of the event that are deemed important for further study.

5. Symbolic Representation: Once students have worked through steps 2–4, they construct symbols to represent these ideas. Through this activity, they begin to better understand the nature of symbol-making, which moves them toward a fuller understanding and discussion of the symbols associated with mathematics. Many students have difficulty understanding the abstractions represented by a discipline's symbols until they experiment with creating symbols for their own ideas.

CHANGES OBSERVED DURING FIRST THREE MONTHS OF THE PROGRAM AT EAGLE HIGH SCHOOL

By the end of the 2006–2007, the differences in student participation in the cohort math class at Eagle were stark between the first six months and the last three months. The last three months, after FCAT preparation, the students were offered the full AP curriculum and pedagogy implemented from March to June 2007. According to Eraso, the observations suggested the following:

- During the three months of AP curriculum, students were more engaged during class time.
- More students participated in group discussions, and more answered questions posed by the teacher.
- For the first six months of instruction with the teacher-on-record, the same three or four students answered questions aloud.
- All students, during AP instruction, were required to stand and present how they had solved a math problem rather than repeating the method of the teacher.

- A class culture of respect and responsibility was developed during AP instruction. Group work continued even when the teacher or assistant was not in the group. Prior to AP, when students were placed in groups, there was no discussion among group members, and in small groups usually two students would work individually to solve the problem, with the other two to three students sitting passively or talking to each other about irrelevant concerns.
- Part of AP's pedagogy is for teachers to give no answers; students must struggle through the problem-solving collaboratively; thus, students became dependent on collective small-group discussion as well as individual critical thinking to solve problems.
- A generally positive group attitude toward fieldtrips, college, and learning developed. Before their field trip to FIU, none had mentioned college as a goal. After the trip, students began to advise others, "If you want to go to college or have a nice living, study."
- Students started to view themselves as a group, capable of moving together and forward in their education. The cohort began reminding each other of why they were studying math and what their ultimate goals were, a departure from the previous sense of isolated individualism observed. The students also began calling to remind each other to bring their parents to monthly AP meetings.
- Students began to volunteer to role-play the mathematician when reading the textbook dialogues. Previously, no one had volunteered.
- Attendance and homework completion improved. From January to March, the attendance was typically twenty students out of twenty-four, with some days as low as eighteen out of twenty-four. After March 19, the average daily attendance was twenty-three out of twenty-four, with many days of perfect attendance. Before March 19 and the inception of the full curriculum and pedagogy of the Algebra Project, average homework completion was one to two students out of twenty-four; after March 19, average homework completion was eight to ten out of twenty-four students.[23]

AP COHORT, 2007–2008 SCHOOL YEAR

Because of students' leaving the neighborhood, the Algebra Project cohort in the beginning of the new school year of 2007–2008 decreased to twenty Eagle students. Records for these twenty students and for a group of twenty students who are similar in academic performance at Eagle were checked, representing their last five years with the system from their middle and high school records.

DEMOGRAPHIC BACKGROUND OF THE AP COHORT

- Three students speak Spanish with limited English proficiency; ten students speak Kreyol and English; three speak Kreyol with limited English proficiency; four speak English and Ebonics.
- Eighteen of the twenty receive free or reduced lunch.
- All twenty students represent those who fall within the lowest FCAT math categories.

The Florida Comprehensive Achievement Test (FCAT) scores are based on a 1 to 5 scale, with 1 being the lowest score and 3 being considered a proficiency score. Seventeen of the cohort scored in a level-1 category, and three of the cohort scored in a level-2 category for the 2005–2006 school year—the year before the intervention. Although typically administered only in the third, eighth, and tenth grades, until a student reaches a score of 3, the student must continue to take the appropriate, grade-specific FCAT every year.

Based upon the math measures data obtained through the Eagle Student Score Database, eighteen of the twenty students have shown gains from the inception of their AP at Eagle. Of the twenty selected students, 25 percent achieved scores that advanced them from the level-1 category to the level-2. One of the three level-2 students in the program shifted in Math Achievement, which allowed her to move into a level-3 category, placing her at the appropriate FCAT proficiency level for her grade. The two remaining level-2 students maintained their level-2 status, although one of the students was able to make gains within that level-2 category.[24]

When measured against a control group, a cohort of twenty students selected on the basis of their comparative likeness on variables such as race, gender, rates of repeating earlier grades, eligibility for free or reduced lunch, and limited English proficiency, the Algebra Project cohort made higher achievements. Only 5 percent of the control group made gains that advanced their level in FCAT math measurement.

THE SUMMER COMPONENT OF THE ALGEBRA PROJECT COHORT PROGRAM

The 2007 summer institute for the Eagle cohort was initiated as a result of lessons learned from the previous years in Mississippi with the AP Lanier High School cohort. Realizing that its Mississippi cohort needed more academic support if they were to be successful in being admitted into college, the Algebra Project in 2005 instituted its first summer program for that cohort at the end of their junior year. The center co-sponsored the institute with Mississippi State University, at the latter's campus. The next year, the center hosted the same cohort for the summer on the FIU campus at the end of the Lanier students' senior year. In the summer of 2007, the center, with funding from the Children's Trust, Inc., hosted its first six-week residential summer institute at the FIU campus for AP students from the ninth-grade Eagle cohort, along with a similar group of students from another high school in the city, Brandon High School. The Brandon students had no previous training with Moses and the Algebra Project. Although twenty-five students from each school were invited, only forty students attended.

The summer program provided the students with a series of courses designed to help them strengthen their mathematics and language skills and to prepare them for college. The academic component of the program included courses in mathematics, communications, reading, and writing circles. Several electives, limited to ten to twelve students per course, were offered: Spanish, computer graphics, yoga, drama and spoken word, film production, photography, visual arts, and basketball. The students were allowed to choose two electives.

This effort was labor-intensive and expensive. We cobbled together funds from many sources, the bulk of which, however, came from the

Children's Trust and the center. The cost to house, feed, and instruct forty students for six weeks amounted to approximately $185,000. Moses, six other professors, one language arts consultant, and one psychologist were involved in the academic pieces of the institute, from FIU; a local community college; City College of New York; and Cornell University. Two reading specialists spent three weeks assessing reading levels and delivered daily instruction to two small groups: one male and one female. Seven other instructors delivered the elective afternoon courses. The intensity of the work and the constant attention to emotional as well as academic needs for forty ninth-graders kept teachers and students fully engaged.

The students met for mathematics class every day, Monday through Friday, for ninety minutes a day. Part of the mathematics course offered to both sets of high school students at different times in the morning were modules in geometry offered by two professors who taught for two full weeks each. A math researcher taught algebra for one full week. Moses taught the mathematics classes for the majority of the summer. These classes were consistently highly rated by the students as superior learning opportunities (see focus group comments below).

While the Brandon students were receiving Action-Research instruction, the Eagle students received a language arts program that included writing circles, peer editing, and linguistic instruction. Students wrote personal stories, learned the international phonetic alphabet and Grimm's Law, and role-played international accents. At the ending summer ceremony with students, instructors, and parents, every student in that course chose to recite in unison linguistic rules and derivations to show the parents what they had learned from the class. The enthusiastic class response to this course resounded through the banquet hall; the written evaluations on the final day of class were equally as enthusiastic, as were the focus group responses about the language arts program.

In the Student Action-Research (SAR) course, students engaged in activities that taught them how to document their successes and challenges in high school. The students said they wished the class could be offered at their school in the fall. Their final products detailed their growth in grappling with self-reflective practices, critical thinking about their learning environment, and knowledge of data collection and analysis.[25]

In addition to these academic classes, students were offered experiences in building social and conflict resolution skills. Every afternoon, small groups divided into male and females met with a psychologist for forty-five minutes. Because the institute was the students' first experience of dormitory life, these sessions became invaluable in learning to work out conflicts during the six weeks.

During the first two days of the summer program, the students attended team-building workshops. These two days were designed as a result of discovering tensions between the two high school groups prior to students' arrival on campus. During several recruiting meetings in the spring, individual students from both schools raised concerns about sharing rooms with participants from the "other" high school. Eagle High's mostly Haitian population lived across town from Brandon High's students, who lived in the oldest African American neighborhood in the city. Both sets of students lacked any sense of trust or safety about the other set. Eight students at each school, all of them female, told the graduate researcher that they were afraid to be in the room with girls from the other school, afraid that violence would occur. In fact, a couple of weeks before the program began, after meeting with students and parents to explain the institute's goals and activities, the fears and mistrust between the schools became so palpable that we began to wonder whether inviting two schools with such intense rivalries had been a good idea. And certainly the first week of the institute was a trial by fire! Student and classroom conflict abounded, but by the end of the second week, life settled and students began taking on the responsibility of holding each other accountable for appropriate behavior.

Five chaperones, recruited from the AP Mississippi graduates, played a key role in reducing students' fears of dormitory life, negotiating interpersonal conflicts, and assisting with academic classes. The chaperones received a standing ovation at the ending banquet.

FOCUS GROUP INTERVIEWS

On the last day of the institute, Janice Giles, an FIU PhD student researcher, interviewed two separate focus groups consisting of seven students from each high school for two hours each. The students were asked what parts of the institute they would like to change, what parts they thought were valuable, why they had chosen to come to the institute, how their parents felt about the experience, and whether they would choose to come again if the institute were offered the following summer. A final question asked, hypothetically, if they were to attend a meeting with local foundations, how they might persuade the foundation that its money would be well spent in funding another three years of summer institutes.

The students' overwhelming response to the institute was positive. Both focus groups unanimously said they wanted the next summer to be twelve weeks instead of six weeks. Several said that they wished the institute could become "a year-long school." Some of the most telling responses came from several students who attended Brandon High School, especially when asked, "What would you say to possible funders for next year's summer institute to persuade them that this effort is worth their support?"

"First thing I'd say," said one student, "is too much kids is dying where I live. While I was here, there were four, no three people got shot and two died. . . . And those kids, those two that died were in my face telling me good-bye on the last day of school, hugged me . . . killed at a school party. If I had not been here, that could have been me, that could have been me. . . . I'm glad that I'm not there. I'm here learning something. All the kids here are learning."

Another chimed in saying, "One of them killed—I knew since I was in third grade; the boy was smart, but he decided to drop out, and if we had more programs like this, people wouldn't drop out. We learned stuff. I swear to God."[26]

All the students from both focus groups said consistently that they had "learned more math in these six weeks" than in their nine years in schools. The Brandon students, who prior to the summer had not known Moses, and who in the beginning weeks found his instruction too rigorous, all mentioned during the interviews how much they had learned from him and the other mathematicians. They all commented on the surprise of learning about geometry through designing "pop-up" books with the mechanical engineer from CCNY and about learning math theories from the Cornell geometer, about creating one-dimensional geometric shapes, which they later connected to make one huge hyperbolic soccer-ball shape. Through these experiences, they learned about positive and zero curvatures and the constant negative curvatures of heptagons.

Another component of the summer that students applauded was the small group life skills sessions led by Dr. Gaynor. One student described the sessions as a surprise: "I hated them at first. I thought, 'What is this woman doing, asking all of those questions, in my face, in my business?' I just clammed up and didn't say a word. But after two sessions, I started lovin' goin' there. She helped us talk to each other in a positive way, even when we were mad at each other." Commenting further, another student said, "I wish our school had ten Dr. Gaynors. Counselors at our school don't help us solve problems. They don't even know us." All students rated the group sessions as one of their favorite experiences.

Students made equally enthusiastic comments about all of the academic courses offered. All of the electives involving movement as well as the Spanish immersion class were mentioned as particularly enjoyable. The only two consistent student criticisms about the institute were that it was not long enough and that late night room-checks were annoying.

LESSONS LEARNED

Through the collaboration, we have learned a number of valuable lessons for working in tandem with public school systems to create access to and success in colleges for disenfranchised children.

1. Demands of leadership
   - This collaboration necessitated calling upon the leadership of the academic department chairs and deans, as well as the civic community. The role of the university is crucial in sustaining the initiative because of the resources that it offers and its perceived credibility as an agent of academic expertise.
   - The financial support through local community grants and donors is critical to creating enrichment opportunities like the summer institute.
   - Receiving approval from the top echelon of a system is crucial in maintaining the partnership before gaining the program's access to a school. Going up and down the chain of command is often required to move from one piece of the program to

the next. In large systems, a complex set of unwritten procedures seems to exist that are often difficult to ascertain.

- State tests seem to dominate the curriculum and pedagogy of "failing schools." In these schools, teaching for the test becomes not a cliché but a harsh reality in mathematics and language skills courses. (While attempting to explain to our new teaching fellow the dilemma we consistently face in getting cooperation to fully implement the AP process, Moses said, "Reaching our kids in huge urban systems is like the days of Jim Crow in Mississippi, where we had to sneak onto the plantation to reach our people who wanted to vote.")

2. Student Achievement Mechanisms

- Through student evaluations during the summer institute, we now know that for the overall program to succeed, the achievement level of the students in the bottom quartile demands a year-long program of support. Others' research also suggests that it takes three months during the fall semester each year to recoup the academic losses due to summer vacations away from school.[27] Through the success of the non-academic support systems offered during the summer, i.e., group and peer counseling, team building skills, action-research empowerment skills, etc., we've learned that academic press is not enough to shepherd our students toward success in academe. The cognitive and affective domains must be addressed.

- Attention to raising the level of achievement in mathematics is not enough. Through the summer institute, we learned that the students' reading skills fell below state levels.

3. Role of Research Mathematicians

- Regular visits of research mathematicians from universities to the classroom created a consistent grounding of theory into practice and a practice grounded in sound mathematical content. The high school math teachers' working alongside research mathematicians raised the level of content knowledge available for students. One of the challenges of urban mathematics classrooms is the scarcity of teachers with adequate content knowledge.[28]

4. Building Relationships
   - Building relationships with students and their parents, visiting their homes, and hosting parent events are essential. Other research suggests the efficacy of positive relationships between disenfranchised students and their teachers.
   - Because the summer institute produced an intense bonding experience for the cohort, those who did not attend sometimes manifest a sense of being outsiders, a factor that seems to impact their academic performance.
   - Bringing the cohort to the FIU campus to speak to two classes of undergraduate pre-service teachers was a powerful experience not only for the cohort but for the pre-service teachers.[29]

CONCLUSION

We have many more lessons to learn as we work with the local cohort and possibly other cohorts. The data gathered as we continue the work will reveal more about the program; yet we know that student voices are essential in grappling with what we know and what we need to know to imagine a way for total access to and success in college for our children at the bottom. A conversation in one of Alice Walker's novels, *By the Light of My Father's Smile,* suggests the power of these children's stories in conjuring their future:

> You are saying . . . that stories have more room in them than ideas? . . .
>
> That is correct, señor. It is as if ideas are made of blocks. Rigid and hard. And stories are made of a gauze that is elastic. You can almost see through it, so what is beyond is tantalizing. You can't quite make it out; and because the imagination is always moving forward, you yourself are constantly stretching. Stories are the way spirit is exercised.
>
> But surely you people have ideas! I said.
>
> Of course we do. But we know that there is a limit to them. After that, story![30]

We believe that along with shifting the politics of education and influencing the will of the nation to educate all of its children, we must also, as Walker suggests, "stretch our imaginations" to offer the content and instruction that will ensure that all of the country's children can tell stories of academically soaring in schools.

NOTES

1. William Minter, Gail Hovey, and Charles Cobb Jr., eds., *No Easy Victories: African Liberation and American Activists over a Half Century, 1950–2000* (Trenton, NJ: Africa World Press, 2008).

2. Barry Lopez, *Crow and Weasel* (New York: Farrar, Straus and Giroux, 1998), 60.

3. Coleman Barks, trans., *The Soul of Rumi: A New Collection of Ecstatic Poems* (San Francisco: HarperCollins Publishers, 2001).

4. Linda Smith, *Decolonizing Methodologies: Research and Indigenous Peoples* (London: Zed Books Ltd., 1999), 1–18.

5. Ibid., 1.

6. Associated Press, "Analysis: Florida Drop-Out Rates High," FloridaToday .com, http://floridatoday.com/ (accessed October 30, 2007).

7. "Robert Moses and the Algebra Project," interview by David Brancaccio, *NOW with David Brancaccio,* PBS, July 15, 2007.

8. Charles Payne, "So Much Reform, So Little Change: Building-level Obstacles to School Change," in *Education Policy for the 21st Century: Challenges and Opportunities in Standards-based Reform,* ed. Lawrence B. Joseph (Chicago: Center for Urban Research and Policy Studies, 2001), 239–78.

9. Joan Wynne, "The Elephant in the Classroom: Racism in School Reform," in *International Perspectives on Methods of Improving Education: Focusing on the Quality of Diversity,* ed. Rose Marie Duhon-Sells (New York: Edwin Mellon Press, 2003), 114–56.

10. Payne, "So Much Reform, So Little Change."

11. Robert Moses and Charles C. Cobb, *Radical Equations: Civil Rights from Mississippi to the Algebra Project* (Boston: Beacon Press, 2001), 18–21.

12. "Robert Moses and the Algebra Project," PBS.

13. Moses and Cobb, *Radical Equations.*

14. Ibid., 19.

15. Pauline Lipman, *Race, Class, and Power in School Restructuring* (Albany: State University of New York Press, 1999).

16. Mary West and Frank Davis, *The Algebra Project at Lanier High School, Jackson, MS* (Cambridge, MA: Lesley University Program Evaluation and Research Group, 2004).

17. Mary West and Frank Davis, *The Algebra Project's High School Initiative: An Evaluation of the First Steps* (Cambridge, MA: Lesley University Program Evaluation and Research Group, 2006).

18. West and Davis, *The Algebra Project at Lanier High School.*

19. [Confidential] County Public Schools Statistical Abstract, 2006–2007. [Confidential URL] (accessed September 2007) [Confidential] County Public Schools individual school databank. 2006. [Confidential High School] (student databank made available only through high school administrators). Information acquired through scores and data distributed to students on [Confidential] test results student scorecard. Information acquired through the [Confidential] Student Score Database.

20. Mario Eraso, Field notes, 2006–07.

21. Ibid.

22. Moses and Cobb, *Radical Equations*, 120–24.

23. Eraso, Field notes.

24. [Confidential] County Public Schools Statistical Abstract, 2006–2007.

25. Alison Cook-Sather, "Sound, Presence, and Power: 'Student Voice' in Educational Research and Reform," *Curriculum Inquiry* 36 (2006), 359–90.

26. Focus group video, conducted by Janice Giles, Center for Urban Education and Innovation, Florida International University, 2007.

27. Harris Cooper, "Summer Learning Loss: The Problem and Some Solutions," *ERIC Digest:* ED475391 (2003); Kathy Christie, "Making Use of Summer Time," in *Phi Delta Kappan* 84, no. 7 (March 2003), 485-87, http://www.ecs.org (accessed March 2003); "Planning for Summer School: A Tool to Help Students Achieve High Standards," in *The Informed Educator* (Arlington, VA: Education Research Services, 2000).

28. William Schmidt et al., *The Preparation Gap: Teacher Education for Middle School Mathematics in Six Countries* (MT21 Report) (Michigan State University College of Education, 2007). Available at http://www.educ.msu.edu/content/sites/usteds/documents/MT21Report.pdf.

29. Theresa Perry, Claude Steele, and Asa G. Hilliard III, *Young, Gifted, and Black: Promoting High Achievement among African-American Students* (Boston: Beacon Press, 2003); Asa G. Hilliard III, "Awaken the Geniuses of Children: The Nurture of Nature," unpublished speech for Skylight 6th International Teaching for Intelligence Conference, 2000 (cassette produced by Chesapeake Audio/Video Communications, 6330 Howard Lane, Elkridge, MD 21075 [00227–1160]); Wanda Blanchard and Joan Wynne, "Reframing Urban Education Discourse: A Conversation with and for Teacher Educators," *Theory into Practice* 46 (2007): 187–94.

30. Alice Walker, *By the Light of My Father's Smile* (New York: Random House, 1998).

FURTHER REFERENCES

Frank Davis, "Transactions of Mathematical Knowledge in the Algebra Project," in *Improving Access to Mathematics: Diversity and Equity in the Classroom,* N. S. Nasir and P. Cobb, eds. (New York: Teachers College Press, 2006), 69–88.

Frank Davis and Mary West, *The Impact of the Algebra Project on Mathematics Achievement* (Cambridge, MA: Program Evaluation and Research Group, Lesley University, 2000).

Joanne Dowdy and Joan Wynne, eds., *Racism, Research, and Educational Reform: Voices from the City* (New York: Peter Lang, 2005).

Robert Moses, Frank Davis, and Mary West, "Culturally Responsive Education: The Algebra Project," in *Culturally Responsive Mathematics Education* (New York: Routledge, 2009), 239–56.

Mary West et al., *The Algebra Project's Middle School Intervention in 1997–98* (Cambridge, MA: Program Evaluation and Research Group, Lesley University, 1998).

9

Culturally Responsive Pedagogies

Lessons from Teachers

Lisa Delpit

When I teach worn-out new teachers every Thursday at five thirty in the evening, it breaks my heart to see the stress outlined around their eyes and the corners of their mouths. They seem so tired. On some days, some of them have been crying. I have come to know about their own children who make demands on their nonexistent time. I have come to know about their ailing parents for whom they are the sole caretakers, about their husbands who have had heart attacks, about their upcoming marriages or divorces, about the problematic pregnancies they are experiencing, or about the new babies who catch cold after cold.

And then I hear about the parents of their students who "don't care" and about the children who are disrespectful or uninterested, who cannot read, who constantly talk, and who always get into fights. And although my heart aches for the difficulties these hardworking teachers are facing, I find I must challenge their interpretations of the children and their parents and challenge them to look beyond what they think they see in parents and students to what they may see in themselves. I find I must add what must initially seem like more stress to their already stressful lives as I ask them to change their patterns of behavior and dig deep to become the teachers I know they can be—the teachers who can change the lives of the poor children of color that they teach and, subsequently, the failing schools of this country's cities.

There is much talk about the "problem" of urban education, much research to study the problem, many policies enacted to address the problem, but little belief that anything will ever really change. After all, that little voice constantly asserts itself between the lines of the research reports, the policy documents, and the energetic beginning-of-school pep talks, saying we cannot change the community, we cannot change the parents, we cannot change the crime, the drugs, the violence. But despite mutterings to the contrary, I know that there are things that we can do, because I have seen them make a difference. I have seen children who, based on their socioeconomic status or their ethnicity, were expected to score at the bottom of their respective districts on standardized tests score, instead, in the top 10 percent of their state. Educators have proven this over and over again. For example, the Marcus Garvey School in Los Angeles, California; the Chick School in Kansas City, Missouri; Harmony-Leland in Cobb County, Georgia; and the Prescott School in Oakland, California, among many others, have all educated low-income African American children who have performed at higher levels on mandated standardized tests than schools serving the most affluent students in their respective districts.[1]

Sankofa Shule, a public, African-centered charter school in Michigan, has produced low-income African American students who are reading from two to four levels above grade level, who are doing algebra and calculus in grade school, and who outscored Lansing School District and the state of Michigan on the state accountability test (the MEAP) in 2000 in mathematics and writing. The school was called "an educational powerhouse" by *U.S. News & World Report* in its April 27, 1998, issue.[2]

When I share this information with my young teachers, I try to help them understand what needs to happen in schools to approach such results. They, like most others in the educational enterprise, tend to believe that there is some magic program out there that will solve their problems. My friend and colleague Martha Demientieff, a gifted Alaska Native teacher, says that we all seem to be waiting for some new program to ride in on a white horse and save us!

The reality is that we can actually save the children we teach and ourselves, regardless of which instructional program we adopt. With changes in attitudes and actions in classrooms, without the need for outside experts, we can change what happens in schools and we can change the lives of our students. I have tried to talk about these changes in ways teachers find not so overwhelming. The following is my attempt to codify the information gleaned from my own teaching, from my colleagues' or my own research, and most important, from what I have learned from watching and talking with extraordinary teachers who regularly perform magic. These teachers have taught me the following lessons.

SEE THEIR BRILLIANCE: DO NOT TEACH LESS CONTENT TO POOR, URBAN CHILDREN; INSTEAD, TEACH MORE!

So often in the belief that we are "being nice," we fail to realize the brilliance of our students and teach down to them, demanding little. In an insightful study titled "Racism Without Racists: Institutional Racism in Urban Schools," researchers Massey, Scott, and Dornbush found that under the pressures of teaching and with all intentions of being kind, teachers had essentially stopped attempting to teach Black children.[3] They showed how oppression could arise out of warmth, friendliness, and concern, through a lack of challenging curricula and evaluation. Carter G. Woodson wrote in his book *The Mis-Education of the Negro,*

> The teaching of arithmetic in the fifth grade in a backward county in Mississippi should mean one thing in the negro school and a decidedly different thing in the white school. The negro children as a rule come from the home of tenants and peons who have to migrate annually from plantation to plantation looking for light which they have never seen. The children from the homes of white planters and merchants live permanently in the midst of calculations, family budgets, and the like which enables them sometimes to learn more through contact than a negro can acquire in school. Instead of teaching such children less arithmetic, we must teach them more than white children.[4]

As in Woodson's world of 1933, today's middle-class children acquire a great deal of school knowledge at home. Those children who do not come from middle-class families must be taught more to catch up. If children come to us knowing less, and we put them on a track of slower paced, remedial learning, then where will they end up?

Teaching to state-mandated tests exacerbates this problem. By illustration, when I visited a small, private school, the three- and four-year-olds ran up to me, eager to share what they had learned that week. They showed me pictures and told me all about the structure of the middle ear. One of them had a hearing loss, so they were all studying what that meant. They could name all the parts of the ear and told me how the brain processed sound. When I went up to the first- and second-grade classroom, those children, too, were eager to share. They were studying the constellations and had taken a trip to the planetarium so that they could learn to identify them in the night sky. They were learning the stories and myths that several cultures connected with various constellations. They were also writing their own myths about the star patterns they saw at night.

When I go to inner-city schools, the children are just as excited to share their work. However, they show me their handwriting papers, their test-oriented workbook pages on subject-verb agreement, or their multiple-choice responses to reading comprehension paragraphs. These latter children may well improve their scores on the state-mandated tests that ask them to prove they know such things, but which children are receiving a better education? Which will have discovered information that will give them the opportunity to become doctors, astronomers, or writers? Which ones are likely to have the background information college texts will demand?

ENSURE THAT ALL CHILDREN GAIN ACCESS TO BASIC SKILLS—THE CONVENTIONS AND STRATEGIES THAT ARE ESSENTIAL TO SUCCESS IN AMERICAN SOCIETY.

What we call basic skills are typically the linguistic conventions of middle-class society and the strategies successful people use to access new information. For example, punctuation, grammar, specialized subject vocabulary, mathematical operations, five-paragraph essays, and so forth are all conventions. Using phonetic cues to read words, knowing how to solve word problems, determining an author's purpose, and finding meaning in context are all strategies. All children need to know these things. Some learn them being read to at home.

Some learn them writing thank-you notes for their birthday presents under their parents' tutelage. Some learn them, as Woodson suggested, just living in a middle-class home environment.[5] Those who do not learn them before they come to school depend on school to teach them.

But this does not mean that we can do so by teaching decontextualized bits of material and expect children to learn how to function in the world. Answering fill-in-the-blank questions or focusing solely on the minutiae of learning will not create educated people.

One evening when my daughter was in first grade, she had a homework assignment to write three sentences. She was a child who loved to write, so I did not anticipate any problems with the assignment. We discussed topics she could write about—her grandmother's upcoming visit, her recent birthday party, or the antics of her two new kittens. As she began to write, the telephone rang, and I walked away to answer it. After finishing the phone call, I came back to see how she was doing. She informed me that she was finished and gave me her notebook to read what she had written—"The dog can run. The boy is tall. The man is fat."

I was puzzled by the lack of any personal significance in her words and finally responded, "That's really great, Maya, but what happened to writing about your grandmother or the party or the kittens?" My six-year-old looked patiently at me and said with great deliberateness, "But Mom, I'm supposed to write sentences!" Still trying to get a handle on her perspective, I asked, "Maya, what are sentences?" She responded quickly, "Oh you know, Mom, stuff you write but you never would say." Ah, so.

This teacher had, I am sure inadvertently, taught that sentences were meaningless, decontextualized statements you find in workbooks and on the blackboard, sentences that "you never would say." Written work in school was not connected to anything real, certainly not to real language. As all good, experienced teachers know, there are many ways to make school feel like it is a part of real life. Spelling words can be taken from stories children write in invented spelling. Grammar conventions can be taught as they arise in the letters children can write to their sports heroes or in the plays they might write to perform for the class. Strategies can be taught in the context of solving community problems, building model rockets, reading the directions for new board games, or learning to summarize and simplify a concept into a form appropriate for teaching it to a younger child. Strategies and conventions must be taught, but they must be taught within contexts that provide meaning.

WHATEVER METHODOLOGY OR INSTRUCTIONAL PROGRAM YOU USE, DEMAND CRITICAL THINKING.

There is evidence that a number of instructional approaches may work for children in urban settings who might not be expected to succeed. Whatever approach or methodology is implemented, however, one factor that is necessary for excellence is that children are demanded to think critically about what they are learning and about the world at large. A key word here is *demand*. Many times it will not initially feel comfortable for students who have previously been asked solely to complete workbook pages. Yet many children, especially African American children, need and expect the teacher to push them. "To," as one young African American man said, "make me learn."

Famed mathematics teacher Dr. Abdulahim Shabazz has successfully taught students who came to college with deficits in mathematics at three historically Black universities. During the period from 1956 to 1963, while he was chair of the mathematics department at Atlanta University, 109 students graduated with master's degrees in math. More than one third of those went on to earn doctorates in mathematics or math education from some of the best universities in the United States. Many of the original 109 produced students who earned PhDs in math. Nearly 50 percent of the African American PhD mathematicians in 1990 in the United States (about 200) resulted in some way from the original 109 Shabazz master's students.[6] Shabazz says that a significant percentage of the original 109 began with serious academic deficits in math and language arts. His slogan has always been, "Give me your worst ones and I will teach them." How has he done this?

In an interview with Dr. Asa Hilliard,[7] Shabazz made it clear that SAT and ACT scores have almost no meaning for him. Instead, he has focused on a set of excellence-level goals that have shaped his approach to dealing with all students. His goals are

- to teach understanding rather than merely to teach mathematical operations;
- to teach mathematical language for the purpose of communicating in mathematics and not merely as a way to solve textbook problems;
- to teach students that math is not at all a fixed body of knowledge but that it is an experimental enterprise in the truest sense of that word and that their approach to the solution of mathematical problems then and in the future should be to try a variety of strategies;
- to have students believe as he does that mathematics "is nothing more than a reflection of life and that life itself is mathematical." He wants them to know that the symbols used in mathematics approximate the reality of human experience and cosmic operations;
- to give his students a sense of hope that they can become superior performers.[8]

This is a testament to demanding critical thinking—not to accept anything as a given but to understand one's own agency in the process of education and connect teaching and learning to the students' own worlds. Other successful teachers have adopted various versions of this thinking strategy in their own subject areas and to students of varying ages. Carrie Secret, a phenomenal teacher of low-income African American elementary students in California, presents complex material to her charges by reading to them and having them listen to recordings of famous African American speakers. In one series of lessons, she has third-graders recreate a sermon of the famous minister Jeremiah Wright as a dramatic performance. The sermon is not written for children and is full of difficult vocabulary and complex metaphorical allusions. She and the children define the vocabulary together, delve into the metaphors, and explore the meaning of each line of the often complicated text. The students write about how the text connects to their own lives and explore how the messages in the sermon connect to other literature they have studied. Only after exhaustive study do the children then perform the text for parents and other adults. I have seen one of their performances and know firsthand why they routinely move their audiences to standing ovations, shouts of approval, and tears of pride. These children know what they are talking about, know what it means to them, and know how to make others believe it.

Although we sometimes seem to act to the contrary, there is no real dichotomy between teaching basic skills and insisting that children learn to think critically. As with Shabazz's and Secret's students, when we teach appropriate conventions and strategies within the context of critical thinking, we can produce the educated people we strive for. To quote my own previously published work,

> A "skilled" minority person who is not also capable of critical analysis becomes the trainable, low-level functionary of the dominant society, simply the grease that keeps the institutions which orchestrate his or her oppression running smoothly. On the other hand, a critical thinker who lacks the "skills" demanded by employers and institutions of higher learning can aspire to financial and social status only within the disenfranchised underworld.[9]

PROVIDE THE EMOTIONAL EGO STRENGTH TO CHALLENGE RACIST SOCIETAL VIEWS OF THE COMPETENCE AND WORTHINESS OF THE CHILDREN AND THEIR FAMILIES.

Children are particularly susceptible to the media's assaults on the intelligence, morality, and motivation of people who look like them. The general notion in this country is that children who belong to stigmatized groups are "less than" their middle-class, lighter skinned age-mates. Children readily internalize these beliefs about themselves. I was once working with a young girl who had failed to learn multiplication. When I announced my intention to work with her on the topic, she looked at me and said, "Ms. Lisa, why are you doing this? Black people don't multiply, they just add and subtract. White people multiply." Were it not for the poignancy of her statement, it would be funny. Here is a child who set severe limits on her potential based on a misguided notion of the limits of African Americans, a notion no doubt appropriated from the larger American culture. She had never been told that Africans created much of what we know as higher mathematics. She knew none of the great African American scientists and engineers.

It reminded me of my own nephew, who is only six years younger than I am—a difference great enough that I had experienced most of my early schooling in segregated schools, whereas he attended only schools that had officially been desegregated. When he was in high school and I was just out of college, I once berated him for making a D in chemistry. His response was, "What do you want from me? The White kids get Cs!" Although I had internalized the notion that we Black kids had to be "twice as good as White kids to get half as far," as had been drilled into us by parents and teachers in all-Black schools, he could not imagine that he could and should be equal to, if not better than, his White classmates.

In *Young, Gifted, and Black: Promoting High Achievement Among African-American Students,* Theresa Perry points out that although there was no expectation of being rewarded for advanced education in the same ways as Whites in the larger society were, African Americans from slavery through the civil rights movement pursued educational achievement with a vengeance. In an attempt to develop a theory of Black achievement, Perry offered an analysis of why education was such a clear goal for educational attainment in the past and why that goal has become so much murkier in today's society. Perry argued that because the country's dominant belief system has always denigrated the academic competence and capacity of African Americans—most overtly visible in Jim Crow and the pre–civil rights era—Black institutions of the past, including segregated schools, organized themselves to counter this hegemonic belief:

> Most, if not all of the historically Black segregated schools that African-American children attended were intentionally organized in opposition to the ideology of Black inferiority. In other words, in addition to being sites of learning, they also instituted practices and expected behaviors and outcomes that not only promoted education—an act of insurgency in its own right—but also were designed to counter the ideology of African-Americans' intellectual inferiority and ideologies that saw African-Americans as not quite equal and

as less than human. Everything about these institutions was supposed to affirm Black humanity, Black intelligence, and Black achievement.[10]

In Black schools, churches, clubs—indeed, all Black community institutions—everything focused on this one goal. In all settings, there were intentional activities and belief systems designed to ensure achievement, including regularly practiced rituals that included uplifting songs, recitations, and performances; high expectations; extensive academic support in and out of school; and regular group meetings to express the expectations of adults that young people must work hard to be free in an oppressive society.

Today's schools, integrated or not, seldom develop the same kind of intentional communities. In the post–civil rights era, most public schools are de-ritualized institutions. Certainly, they are institutions that are not intentionally organized to counter inferiority myths— and the reality is, because of that kind of institutional space, Black students today, as perhaps never before, are victims of the myths of inferiority and find much less support for countering these myths and embracing academic achievement outside of individual families.

When I spoke at Southern University a few years ago, a young African American woman who had been a student teacher the semester before told me that one of her students, a young African American teenager, came up to her after a social studies lesson and said, "So, Ms. Summer, they made us the slaves because we were dumb, right?" She had been so hurt by his words that she did not know how to respond.

To teach children who have internalized racist beliefs about themselves, one of the things that successful teachers must constantly say to them is, "You will learn! I know you will learn because you are brilliant." Jamie Escalante taught poor barrio children in California to pass advanced placement calculus tests. As depicted in the movie *Stand and Deliver,* he would say to them, "You have to learn math. Math is in your blood. The Mayans discovered zero!"[11]

We have to be able to say to our children that we understand and they need to understand that this system is set up to guarantee their failure. To succeed in school is to cheat the system, and we are going to spend our time cheating. Teachers have an important role to play here. They must not only make children aware of the brilliance "in their blood" but also help children turn any internalized negative societal view of their competence into a compelling drive to demand that any system attempting to relegate them to the bottom of society must, instead, recognize and celebrate their giftedness.

RECOGNIZE AND BUILD ON CHILDREN'S STRENGTHS.

To do this requires knowledge of children's out-of-school lives. One of the teachers in Gloria Ladson-Billings's *The Dreamkeepers* (1994) speaks of having brought candy to school for a holiday party.[12] She thought she brought enough candy for everyone, but all of the candy disappeared before half the children had been served. She was perplexed but then discovered that the children were putting some of the candy in their pockets. After some inquiries, she realized that they were doing so to take some home for their siblings. Many teachers might end any inquiries about the disappearing candy with the conclusion that the children were stealing. They might think, "I'm not going to bring candy into this classroom anymore because these children are selfish and untrustworthy." But this teacher understood that what was happening was a real strength that she could build on. After all, how many children from middle-class families would be so focused on making sure that siblings received the same treats that they did? These children were exhibiting a sense of caring for others and nurturing that could very well make instructional strategies such as peer tutoring or collaborative learning much easier to implement.

When I was a new teacher, Howard was a first-grader in my class. After several months of failing to get Howard to progress in mathematics, I was ready to take the advice I was given to refer him for special education placement. Among other academic problems, Howard was having real difficulty with math worksheets, especially those concerning money, on which there are pictures of different configurations of coins and the child is supposed to indicate the total amount represented. It did not seem to matter how frequently we reviewed those worksheets, Howard just could not get it. Before I made any referrals, I had the opportunity to visit Howard's home and talk to his mother and his grandmother. I found out that Howard's mother was suffering with a substance addiction and that Howard was responsible for getting his four-year-old physically challenged sister up every morning and on the bus to school. He also did the family's wash, which meant that he had to have a lot of knowledge about coins and money. He was very good at it because he knew he could not get cheated when he purchased laundry supplies from the corner store. What I found out through that experience was that I, without really knowing this child, almost made a terrible mistake. I assumed that because he could not do a task in my classroom that was decontextualized and paperbound, he could not do the real-life task it represented. It is often very difficult for teachers, particularly those who may not be from the same cultural or class background as the children, to understand where strengths may lie. We must have means to discover what the children are able to do outside of school—in church, at community centers, as caretakers for younger siblings—or what skills they may be able to display on the playground with their peers. Many of our youngsters in urban settings come to us with what we refer to as "street smarts," yet we seldom seem able to connect that kind of knowledge to school problem-solving and advanced thinking.

USE FAMILIAR METAPHORS, ANALOGIES, AND EXPERIENCES FROM THE CHILDREN'S WORLD TO CONNECT WHAT CHILDREN ALREADY KNOW TO SCHOOL KNOWLEDGE.

To connect students' out-of-school lives to academic content, another teacher described in *The Dreamkeepers* taught about the governmental structure of the United States by connecting it to the Black church structure.[13] She had the children collect the articles of incorporation of their churches. She then made the connection to show how the minister could be compared to the president, how the deacons could be compared to the legislators, and how the board could be compared to the senators. The children not only learned about the constitution in a way that they were able to apprehend with much greater clarity but also learned that institution building was not merely the purview of others but a part of their culture as well.

Yet another teacher, Amanda Branscombe, who is European American, had a class of ninth-graders who were considered special education students. She had the children teach her the rules for writing a rap song. She told them, "No, no, you can't just tell me to write it, you have to tell me the rules. I know nothing about rap songs. I've never even heard one. What rules do I need to know to write one?" So the children really had to explore meter, verse, and the structure of a rap song. After they had done so—and that was a massive undertaking on its own—Branscombe compared their rules to those Shakespeare used to write his sonnets. Then they set about exploring Shakespeare's rules in the context of his writing.[14]

One year my mother, who was a teacher, taught plane geometry by having the students make a quilt for a student who had dropped out of school to get married and have a baby. The students presented this quilt to this young woman as a present. There are several connections here. It is obvious that by making the quilt, the students were creating something for someone they cared about, but their teacher also taught them the theorems of geometry as they worked to piece the shapes of the quilt together. School knowledge was connected to a sense of community. Teachers really are cultural brokers who have the opportunity to connect the familiar to the unknown. We teachers have to work at learning to do that.

CREATE A SENSE OF FAMILY AND CARING IN THE SERVICE OF ACADEMIC ACHIEVEMENT.

Jackie Irvine, a friend and colleague, told me about her interview with a teacher identified as an excellent teacher of African American children. She asked Ms. Brandon (not her real name), "How do you view teaching? How do you ensure children's success?" The teacher answered, "Well, the first thing I have to do is make the children mine." She continued, saying that on the first day of school she would go down each row and say "Son, what is your name?" The little boy would say, "My name is Justin Williams." And she would say, "Sweetheart, that is a wonderful name, but in this class your name is going to be Justin Williams Brandon." She would ask the next child, "Darling, what's your name?" "My name is Mary Johnson." She would say,

"And in this class, darling, your name is Mary Johnson Brandon." Ms. Brandon proceeded down each row to give each child her last name. She then said, "Now, you are all my children, and I have the smartest children in the entire world. So you are going to learn more this year than anybody ever learned in one year. And we are going to get started right now."

In her dissertation research, Madge Willis looked at a very successful school in Atlanta serving low-income African American students and found an overwhelming sense of family, a sense of connectedness, and a sense of caring.[15] I have discovered that children of color, particularly African American children, seem especially sensitive to their relationship between themselves and their teacher. I have concluded that it appears that they not only learn from a teacher but also for a teacher. If they do not feel connected to a teacher on an emotional level, then they will not learn; they will not put forth the effort.

Barbara Shade suggests that African American children value the social aspects of an environment to a greater extent than "mainstream" children and tend to put an emphasis on feelings, acceptance, and emotional closeness. Shade contends that the time and effort African American children will spend on academic tasks in a classroom depend on their interpretation of the emotional environment.[16]

MONITOR AND ASSESS CHILDREN'S NEEDS AND THEN ADDRESS THEM WITH A WEALTH OF DIVERSE STRATEGIES.

We do a lot of monitoring and assessing, of course, but we are not very adept at addressing specific needs, especially in diverse cultures. Assessment in these contexts is not as straightforward as it may seem on the surface. In her studies of the narrative styles of young children, Sarah Michaels found that Black and White first graders tended to tell "sharing time" stories differently. White children tended to tell "topic-centered" stories, focused on a single object or event, whereas Black children tended to tell "episodic" stories, usually longer and always including shifting scenes related to a series of events.[17] In a subsequent study, Courtney Cazden and Sarah Michaels created a tape of a White adult reading the oral narratives of Black and White first-graders with all dialectal markers removed. They then played the tape for a racially mixed group of educators and asked each educator to comment about the children's likelihood of success in school. The researchers were surprised by the differential responses of African American and European American educators to an African American child's story.[18]

The White adults' comments included statements such as these:

"Terrible story, incoherent."

"Not a story at all in the sense of describing something that happened."

"This child might have trouble reading."

"This child exhibits language problems that will affect school achievement; family problems or emotional problems might hamper academic progress."[19]

By contrast, the African American adults found the story "well-formed, easy to understand, and interesting, with lots of detail and description."[20] All five of the African American adults mentioned the "shifts" and "associations" or "nonlinear" qualities of the story, but they did not find this distracting. Three of the five African American adults selected this story as the best of the five they heard. All but one judged the child as exceptionally bright, highly verbal, and/or potentially successful.

This is not a story about racism. Again, there was no way that the adults knew the race of the child who told the story, because all the stories were read by a White researcher. The point here is that when a teacher is familiar with aspects of a child's culture, then the teacher may be better able to assess the child's competence. Many teachers, unfamiliar with the language, the metaphors, or the environments of the children they teach, may easily underestimate the children's competence.

I have also discovered that to effectively monitor and assess the needs of children who come from a different cultural background, the notion of basic skills often needs to be turned on its head. We must constantly be aware that children come to school with different kinds of knowledge. Our instruction must be geared toward understanding that knowledge, building on it, and teaching that which children do not already know. To offer appropriate instruction, we need to understand that because what we typically think of as basic skills are those skills that middle-class children learn before they come to school—knowledge of letter names and sounds, color names, and counting; recognition of numerals; familiarity with storybooks and with the particular kinds of language found in them; and so forth. Those skills may not be basic to children from nonmainstream or non–middle-class backgrounds. We also need to rethink the general belief that critical and creative thinking, the ability to analyze, and the ability to make comparisons and judgments are higher-order skills. It is often the case that for children who are from poor communities, critical thinking skills are basic. Those are the skills they come to us with. They are accustomed to being more independent. Often they are familiar with real-life problems and how to solve them.

So those children who appear to learn the basic skills presented in school quickly typically learn most of them during their five or six years at home. Low-income children who did not learn these skills at home, and who do not learn them in the first five or six months of school, are often labeled remedial at best or special education material at worst. Even more problematic, the knowledge that these children do come to school with is often viewed as a deficit rather than an advantage. I have seen far too many children labeled as "too street-wise" by adults who see their ability to solve problems with near adult sophistication as violating some preconceived notion of childhood innocence.

An Anglo teacher I worked with in Alaska successfully taught low-income Alaska Native children in rural villages. When she came to teach in the city, she was appalled at how dependent the middle-class children were. "They don't even know how to tie their shoes," she said of her kindergarten class. The village kindergartners could not only tie their shoes but also fix meals for their siblings, clean up, and help their parents with all sorts of tasks. The village kindergartners, members of an ethnic group typically stigmatized by the larger society, took on the responsibility of keeping areas of the classroom in order with little adult supervision, which freed their teacher to work on academic tasks with small groups. The teacher found the city kids unprepared for such responsibilities. When paint spilled on the floor, most of the middle-class children stood around waiting for someone to clean it up. In the village, the children would take care of the problem without the teacher ever knowing a problem had occurred.

What I am suggesting is that we teach traditional school knowledge to those children for whom basic skills are not so basic and appreciate and make use of the higher order knowledge that they bring from home. On the other hand, I suggest that we appreciate the school knowledge middle-class children bring and teach them the problem-solving and independence that they sometimes lack.

We must also be very aware that we need to use a variety of strategies to teach. Although it is important for children to have the opportunity to discover new knowledge, we must not fool ourselves that children need only, for example, a literacy rich environment to discover literacy. What we seldom realize is that middle-class parents are masters at direct teaching long before their children ever enter school.

I recently visited a child-care center where I saw children pounding nails into a tree trunk and having a great time. When a father arrived to pick up his daughter, she called out to him, "Come see what I'm doing!" The father joined her at the tree trunk to admire her work. The father inquired, "Do you remember what we said those rings in the tree trunk were for? Yes, to tell how old the tree is. Let's count the rings and see how old this tree is." The point here is that if that child were later put into a "tree trunk–rich" environment, it might appear that she discovered the meaning of tree rings on her own. We have to know when to teach information directly and when to provide opportunities for children to explore and discover—and we have to realize the difference between teaching and merely allowing children to display what they have already learned at home.

We have to have a variety of methodologies, we have to be able to assess broadly, and we have to be able to pull out of our teaching hats the appropriate method for the children who are sitting before us at any given moment.

HONOR AND RESPECT THE
CHILDREN'S HOME CULTURE.

When educators hear this precept, they frequently interpret it to mean that they are being directed to create an all–African American or all-Latino or all–Native American curriculum. This is not what is being asked of them. Most parents do want their children to learn about their own culture, but they also want them to learn about the rest of the world. I have described what I want for my child as an academic house built on a strong foundation of self-knowledge but with many windows and doors that look out onto the rest of the world. A problem, however, is that the cultures of marginalized groups in our society tend to be ignored, misrepresented, viewed from an outsider perspective, or even denigrated. Aside from a yearly trek through the units on Martin Luther King Jr. and perhaps Rosa Parks, the historical, cultural, and scientific contributions of African Americans are usually ignored or rendered trivial.

Even when they have the desire to do so, educators are often unable to connect to the cultures of their students because our universities are so limited in what is taught about other cultures. I sometimes ask my students to make a list of the names of an explorer, a philosopher, a scientist, a poet, and a mathematician. After they have completed their lists, I then ask that they write the names of a Chinese explorer, a Latino philosopher, a South American scientist, a Native American poet, and an African mathematician. Obviously, the first list is much easier for them and is usually populated with names of European males. The second list is almost impossible for them to complete. I point out the cultural deficits with which we in this country are typically saddled as a result of our limited education!

Teachers who wish to learn the culture of their students usually have to pursue the study on their own. One excellent example of a teacher who has done so is Stephanie Terry of Baltimore, Maryland. When I visited her classroom, Stephanie taught first-grade in an all–African American school. Although she considered herself an Afrocentric teacher, she taught the curriculum mandated by the Baltimore school system. However, she always added material about the children's cultural heritage as well. When she taught the mandated unit on libraries, for example, she taught about the first major libraries in Africa. When she taught about health, she taught Imhotep, the famous African physician, philosopher, and scientist. She ensured that the children would find people who looked like them in the curriculum. Stephanie's students always scored near the top of any standardized tests administered, yet she never spent a moment "teaching to the test."

On a cautionary note, however, I should mention my observation of the teacher next door to Stephanie's classroom. That teacher also tried to use African American culture in her curriculum, but her manner of talking to the children seemed to militate against their getting any benefits from the enriched curriculum. Although she had done a lot of research to create her curriculum, she said things to the children such as "You see the way you're acting; you could never be Gwendolyn Brooks! You just don't know how to act. You all act like you don't have any sense at all!" and "You all don't even care about all the work I put into this. You don't have any respect. You just need to sit down and stop acting like idiots. I don't even know why I try anything nice with this class! You'll never be anything!"

I happened to be at an assembly later in the week, where the children were watching the presidential inauguration, and the principal asked, "How many of you think you could be president?" It is interesting that all of Stephanie's kids raised their hands. When I looked at the class from the teacher next door, I saw only one or two hands raised. It struck hard that it is not just the curriculum but also the attitudes toward the children that affect what the children believe about themselves. One cannot honor and respect the culture without honoring and respecting the children themselves. To get teachers to consider the wealth and strength of African American cultural contributions to this country, Ladson-Billings has asked teachers to consider what the United States might look like today if African Americans had arrived only recently.[21] There were many thoughtful responses: If African Americans had just immigrated, this country would not have the rich musical heritage provided by blues, jazz, and gospel. The moral conscience of the nation might not have been heightened without the experience of the civil rights movement. The country would be unrecognizable because we may have failed to grow beyond the thirteen original colonies without the labor of enslaved Africans. The point of the exercise was to help teachers keep in mind the value and the contributions of a particular people to this country when we teach their children.

FOSTER A SENSE OF CHILDREN'S CONNECTION TO COMMUNITY—TO SOMETHING GREATER THAN THEMSELVES.

The role of community in education has changed considerably during the years since the desegregation of schools. Prior to desegregation, the Black community played an especially significant role in schools, providing many of the resources the local districts refused to provide.[22] The children of the community were told in no uncertain terms by their parents and their teachers that their role was to excel in school because so many had suffered so that they might be in the position to receive an education. We students were admonished that we must excel for those who had come before us, for our communities, for our descendants, and in short, for all to whom we were connected by kinship or affiliation.

Perry points out that prior to the civil rights movement, although there was no expectation of being rewarded for advanced education in the same ways as Whites in the larger society were, African Americans pursued educational achievement:

> For African Americans, from slavery to the modern civil rights movement . . . you pursued learning because this is how you asserted yourself as a free person; how you claimed your humanity. You pursued learning so you could work for social uplift, for the liberation of your people. You pursued education so you could prepare yourself to lead your people.[23]

Today's students receive a different message. We tell them that they must do well in school for only one purpose—to get a good job. This incentive to succeed is meager, indeed, when compared to the incentive derived from the possibility of disappointing one's community, prior and future generations, and in truth, the entire race! It would behoove us to rethink how we talk to children about education and its purposes. The connection to community, to something greater than our individual selves, can be the force that propels our children to be their best.

In *Urban Sanctuaries,* Milbrey McLaughlin, Merita A. Irby, and Juliet Langman studied urban children who were and those who were not involved in community organizations. What they found is that children who were a part of some community-based group that valued educational achievement tended to be more successful in school. Whether the group was Boy Scouts, a sports team, or a church group, when the children regularly heard adults important to them outside of school and home discuss the importance of school achievement, they pushed themselves harder to excel.[24] It seems that such groups can create a culture of achievement in which children are loath to disappoint their fellow members. Again, the children were able to benefit by identifying with something greater than themselves.

My young Thursday-night teachers have no idea of the power they actually hold. Despite their feeling of inadequacy, of being overwhelmed and undervalued, what they fail to understand is that they have the potential to change the lives of so many children. When I have asked adults who, based on their childhood demographics, should not have but did achieve significant success—those who came from low-income communities, from single-parent families, from the foster care system, or who spent many years in special education classrooms—they have all identified one common factor to explain their accomplishments. Each of these adults attributed his or her success to one or more teachers. All talked about a teacher who was especially encouraging, or who demanded their best, or who convinced them they were more than the larger world believed. Teachers changed their lives, even when the teachers themselves did not realize they were doing so.

And so, when teachers say they feel ineffectual, I remind them of the significant role they can choose to play. The ten precepts above are offered to assist them in that role. By knowing their students and their students' intellectual heritage and using that knowledge in their instruction, by always demanding students' best, by fighting against societal stereotypes, and by helping students understand the important role they can play in changing their communities and the world, teachers truly can revolutionize the education system and save this country, one classroom at a time.

NOTES

1. Asa G. Hilliard III, "No Mystery: Closing the Achievement Gap," in *Young, Gifted, and Black: Promoting High Achievement among African-American Students,* Theresa Perry et al., eds. (Boston: Beacon Press, 2003), 131–65.
2. Cited in unpublished proposal draft, F. Rivers (Baton Rouge, LA, 2003).
3. Grace C. Massey, Mona V. Scott, Sanford M. Dornbusch, "Racism without Racists: Institutional Racism in Urban Schools," *Black Scholar* 7(3) (1975): 2–11.
4. Carter G. Woodson, *The Mis-Education of the Negro* (Chicago: African American Images, 2000; orig. 1933), 4.

5. Ibid.

6. Asa G. Hilliard III, "Do We Have the Will to Educate All Children?" *Educational Leadership* 49, no. 1 (1991): 31–36.

7. Ibid.

8. Ibid., 23.

9. Lisa Delpit, *Other People's Children: Cultural Conflict in the Classroom* (New York: New Press, 1995), 19.

10. Theresa Perry, "Up from the Parched Earth: Toward a Theory of African-American Achievement," in *Young, Gifted and Black: Promoting High Achievement among African-American Students,* Theresa Perry et al., eds. (Boston: Beacon Press, 2003), 88.

11. Ramón Menéndez (director/writer) and Tom Musca (writer), *Stand and Deliver,* motion picture (United States: Warner Bros., 1988).

12. Gloria Ladson-Billings, *The Dreamkeepers* (San Francisco: Jossey-Bass, 1994).

13. Ibid.

14. Amanda Branscombe, personal communication, 1990.

15. Madge Willis, "'We're Family': Creating Success in a Public African American Elementary School," PhD dissertation, Georgia State University, Atlanta, 1995.

16. Barbara Shade, "Ecological Correlates of Educative Style of African American Children," *Journal of Negro Education* 60 (1987): 291–301.

17. Sarah Michaels, "Sharing Time: Children's Narrative Styles and Differential Access to Literacy," *Language in Society* 10 (1981): 423–42.

18. Sarah Michaels and Courtney B. Cazden, "Teacher-Child Collaboration on Oral Preparation for Literacy," in *Acquisition of Literacy: Ethnographic Perspectives,* B. Schieffer, ed. (Norwood, NJ: Ablex, 1986).

19. Ibid.

20. Ibid.

21. Ladson-Billings, *The Dreamkeepers.*

22. Vanessa Siddle Walker, *Their Highest Potential: An African American School Community in the Segregated South* (Chapel Hill: University of North Carolina Press, 1996).

23. Perry, "Up from the Parched Earth," 11.

24. Milbrey W. McLaughlin, Merita A. Irby, and Juliet Langman, *Urban Sanctuaries: Neighborhood Organizations in the Lives and Futures of Inner-City Youth* (San Francisco: Jossey-Bass, 2001).

CONTRIBUTORS

Alicia Carroll has been teaching in the Boston Public Schools since 1997. Since 2006, she has been a teacher developer, mentoring new teachers. She has developed and published thematic curriculum units on *Young Children Learning About Ancient China Through Archeology*; *Ancient Nubia and Egypt*; *Teaching Africa to Young Children;* and, with Bisse Bowman, *Learning to Read Nature's Book*. She received the Boston Superintendent's Award for Outstanding Teaching in 2002. In 2004, she was a Fulbright scholar to Kenya and Tanzania. Based on extensive research, with Lucy Montgomery she has written and is seeking a publisher for a children's book titled *Malindi's Journey,* which is the story of a giraffe brought by African ambassadors to China with the treasure ships of Zheng He, the Chinese Muslim explorer of the fifteenth century.

Ernesto Cortés Jr. is the southwest regional director of the Industrial Areas Foundation (IAF), a network of community organizations that fights for social justice by waging campaigns for living wages, equitable public investments, effective public school reform, and other causes. A native of San Antonio, Texas, Cortés is a graduate of Texas A&M University, where he majored in English and economics, and graduated at the age of nineteen. Now based in Los Angeles, Cortés is invigorating the IAF in that area. In addition to being named a MacArthur Fellow in 1984, Cortés received the H. J. Heinz Award for public policy in 1999. He was a fellow at the John F. Kennedy School of Government's Institute of Politics at Harvard University in 1993, and he was the Martin Luther King Jr. Visiting Professor in the Department of Urban Studies and Planning at the Massachusetts Institute of Technology in 1999.

Lisa Delpit is executive director for the Center for Urban Education and Innovation at Florida International University. Her work has garnered the Antioch College Horace Mann Humanity Alumni Award, the award for Outstanding Contribution to Education from Harvard Graduate School of Education, and a MacArthur "Genius" Fellowship. Notable publications include *The Skin That We Speak: Thoughts on Language and Culture in the Classroom* (edited with Joanne Kilgour Dowdy, 2002), *The Real Ebonics Debate: Power, Language, and the Education of African-American Children* (edited with Theresa Perry, 1998), and *Other People's Children: Cultural Conflict in the Classroom* (1995).

Janice Giles is a doctoral candidate in the field of international and intercultural development education at Florida International University. Born in London, England, of Afro-Caribbean heritage, she immigrated to the United States in 1983 and completed her secondary education in New York. She obtained a bachelor of arts degree from City University of New York, Hunter College, with a double major in Black and Puerto Rican studies, and psychology. She later graduated with a master of arts degree in African studies and research from Howard University in Washington, D.C. Her research interests include education and identity, Black psychology, and African thought and development.

Linda Mizell is assistant professor of education at the University of Colorado at Boulder. She specializes in the history of African American education and in social studies teacher education. Mizell has worked in adult education and training, as a community organizer, and as an elementary school administrator. She is the author of *Think about Racism,* a text for young adult readers, a number of articles on anti-racist teaching practice, the award-winning teacher's guide to the PBS series *Africans in America,* and numerous middle school and high school teaching guides.

Robert P. Moses is one of the leading civil rights icons from the 1960s. He was the former field secretary for the Student Nonviolent Coordinating Committee (SNCC) and the main organizer of the Freedom Summer project, which was intended to end racial disfranchisement. In 1982 he received a MacArthur "Genius" Fellowship and used the money to create the Algebra Project, which serves ten thousand students in twenty-eight cities nationwide and follows the philosophy of grassroots community organizing to promote math literacy. In 2001, with Charles Cobb, Moses published *Radical Equations: Civil Rights from Mississippi to the Algebra Project.*

Jeannie Oakes is the director of education and scholarship at the Ford Foundation. Until fall 2008, she was presidential professor in educational equity at the University of California at Los Angeles Graduate School of Education and Information Studies. Dr. Oakes is the author of twenty scholarly books and monographs, and more than 125 other publications. Her book *Keeping Track: How Schools Structure Inequality* was honored as one of the twentieth century's most influential books on education. Her most recent book, edited with Marisa Saunders, is *Beyond Tracking: Multiple Pathways to College, Career, and Civic Participation.*

Kimberly N. Parker is a doctoral student in the Department of Curriculum and Instruction at the University of Illinois, Urbana-Champaign. Her dissertation is a qualitative study of the participation of Black middle school boys in a book club. She has taught in middle and high school in public, charter, and independent schools. She consults with high schools on the implementation of strategies that support the development of reading and writing fluency among African American students and on the selection and use of texts that motivate African American youth to read and that are bridge texts to canonical literature. She has worked with community-based organizations on the development of book clubs for Black boys and teen mothers. With a group of African American young men, she is co-authoring a book that tells the story of how they became readers and how reading has transformed their lives.

Imani Perry is professor at Princeton University in the Center for African American Studies. Perry is the author of *Prophets of the Hood: Politics and Poetics in Hip Hop* (2004) and the forthcoming *Righteous Hope: The Making and Unmaking of Racial Inequality in the 21st-century United States.* She is also the author of more than two dozen articles, essays, and book chapters on race, law, and cultural studies.

Theresa Perry is professor of Africana studies and education at Simmons College and director of the Simmons College/Beacon Press Race, Democracy, and Education Lecture and Publishing Series. Her publications include *Young, Gifted and Black: Promoting High Achievement Among African-American Students* (with Asa G. Hilliard III, and Claude Steele, 2003), *The Real Ebonics Debate: Power, Language, and the Education of African-American Children* (edited with Lisa Delpit, 1998), *Teaching Malcolm X* (1996), and *Freedom's Plow, Teaching in the Multicultural Classroom* (edited with James W. Fraser, 1993).

Joan T. Wynne is associate director of the Center for Urban Education and Innovation and a professor in the Department of Educational Leadership and Policy Studies at Florida International University. She taught at Morehouse College for fourteen years, where she designed and directed the Benjamin E. Mays Teacher Scholars Program. She also codesigned and directed an Urban Teacher Leadership master's degree program at Georgia State University.

The editors have donated all royalties from this volume to the Young People's Project, Inc. Founded in 1996 by Algebra Project graduates, YPP is a nonprofit organization that uses math literacy as a tool to develop young leaders and organizers who radically change the quality of education and life in their communities so that all children have the opportunity to reach their full human potential. Established and developing sites are located throughout the United States, and at Hamilton College and the University of Michigan.